Trilogy

Trilogy

Poems by

Frank Samperi

A SKYSILL BOOK

ISBN 978-1-907489-11-2

Copyright © 2013 The Estate of Frank Samperi

All rights reserved. No part of this work covered by the copyright hereon may be reproduced or used in any means – graphic, electronic, or mechanical, including copying, recording, taping, or information storage and retrieval systems – without written permission of the publisher.

Preface, introduction, and afterword, copyright © Robert Kelly, Peter O'Leary and Elizabeth Robinson

SKYSILL PRESS
3 Gervase Gardens
Clifton Village
Nottingham   NG11 8LZ

skysillpress.blogspot.com

Contents

Preface by Robert Kelly
vii

Introduction by Peter O'Leary
ix

The Prefiguration
1

Quadrifariam
219

Lumen Gloriae
501

Afterword by Elizabeth Robinson
609

Appendix
613

A Note on the Text
614

Preface

He sat there every night. He said he was studying. The verb excited me—I had never heard an adult use it about anything but some academic exercise. But Frank was studying. From what he said in letters from time to time, he'd be working there in his apartment late at night, two or three in the morning, maybe, while the noise of Second Avenue died down. The East Village: he was in it if not of it. I pictured him at the kitchen table, window open for breeze, bent over his books, a monk or rabbi of the old days in the House of Study.

In his wonderful letters, I learned gradually the curious choir of the masters he studied (he used that word, spoke of "my masters"). Aquinas, Shankaracarya, Dante, and the rich astrosophy that came to him originally from Rudolf Steiner by way of that curious Max Heindel, who inscribed Steiner's teachings (near as I can reckon) in his own Rosicrucian writings. The great Christian philosopher, the great Advaitan Vedantist, the great poet whose work brooded over his own, and the Rosicrucian. He studied the stars and he studied the texts, reasonings, images, the shadows of ideas.

No one in his time or after has been so lucid. In the long, graceful lines of his poems, obedient only to the measures of thought, he demonstrated the music of thinking, language upwelling to bear his investigations into the intelligential, the realm where symbols, angels and hard facts are truly at home. His letters were just as clear—remarkable in a time that relished (I am the worst of sinners) the anguished jive of manifesto and ego-proclamation. Those letters! neatly hand-written, never typed, full of courtesy down to the old-fashioned way of folding a sheet of typing paper in half to make four pages—a folio, in fact—that would be folded over twice more to fit into a small envelope. Then the pages would be numbered 1–3–2–4—again the courtesy, so that the reader of the first page just opens and sees the next page before him. My old aunts wrote their letters that way, and it was old-fashioned even then, but there it was. High courtesy, as Dante might have practiced it, even down to the slightest things: remember your reader, put yourself in his hands, be easy on him.

How easy to read his poems still. On any page (even, or maybe most especially) in his translations of the *Paradise* of his master, we find a man thinking through the things of the world and how humans have used them, we find a man thinking and inviting us to think with him. Not the tumults of imagery I demanded, or Pound's clangor of trochees, just Samperi's long, quiet considering. To consider is *to think with the stars*. Being aware of the ancient world continuous with now, to accept no gap in the texture, no discontinuity the mind can't leap, heal.

I had not known him in New York, and our acquaintance ripened as they say through correspondence. Once I was able to wangle an invitation from the college where I taught, and able to entice Frank to come up for a reading. The reading was all I could have hoped—clear, powerful, without a hint of side or display. I sat with him afterwards in my living room, he on a green loveseat under the window, me across the room. I marveled at him. How utterly unlike the image of crabbed scholar his letters somehow projected. Here was a man in the prime of life, graceful, strong. No hint of hypersensitivity or malaise. Virile—that's the word that came to mind as he sat speaking quietly, lucidly as ever. His body and manner were those of an athlete in late youth (he must have been forty at the time), alert, strong. In him I got to see the virility of the intelligential, so different from the coarseness of the problem-solving "intelligent," the anxiety of the "intellectual." Here was calm and certitude, a potent humility. And those remarkable qualities perdure in his work, work I am very grateful for the chance to preface with my praise. For Samperi was quick to praise, and wrote (at least in our exchanges) negatively about no one. And that too is part of the virility of mind. And that too is what he gives us, through and beyond the poetry, the presence of a mind that dares to stand before us.

—Robert Kelly, Summer 2012

Introduction

No description, however complete and subtle, can adequately paraphrase the experience of reading Frank Samperi's magnificent *Trilogy*. Not even reading each of the three volumes separately accounts for how firmly the cumulative achievement of this poetry impresses itself on the imagination. At once minimal and theologically dense, obscure and crystal clear, abstract and symbol-laden, joyous and melancholy, Samperi's poetry in his *Trilogy* is ultimately *angelic*, laden with divine messages and abiding in a realm that intermediates the worldly and the heavenly. In *The City of God*, Saint Augustine writes, "Those holy angels come to the knowledge of God not by audible words, but by the presence to their souls of immutable truth, of the only-begotten Word of God."[1] The atmosphere of the *Trilogy* throbs with such angelic presence. Because of the theological intensity that at times guides this work, and because of Samperi's frequent summoning of the word "spiritual" throughout, the *Trilogy* can initially appear to readers as something more formal, more doctrinal than it actually is. Rather, these poems seem to me an incredible intuition of paradise refracted through the gauze of the world but focused there into an oracular power the poet's angelic imagination constantly intensifies.

I discovered the *Trilogy* in the summer of 1996. I had been primed by John Taggart's essay, "A Spiritual Definition of Poetry," which I had read for the first time that spring. I had never heard of Samperi before reading Taggart's essay; the samples of Samperi's poetry the essay contained were alluring. But it didn't prepare me for what awaited me when I found a paperback copy of *Quadrifariam* in the book sale at a literature conference in Maine that June. The book itself was physically striking, gorgeously printed in an oblong quarto edition, providing ample blank space for the irradiation of the poems and adorned with a luxurious, abstract stone print by Will Petersen on the cover. The poetry for me was transformative—I felt the hinge on a door long stuck shut suddenly generously oiled. Here was work in the idiom of

---

1. Saint Augustine, *The City of God* XI:29, translated by Marcus Dods, D.D. (New York: The Modern Library Classics, 2000), p. 374.

the New American Poetry that was not only open to the spiritual but explicitly religious in a way that spoke to another tradition with which I wrestled, Catholicism. The book quickly became a treasure. And in the days before internet book searches, I devoted myself to finding copies of the opening and closing volumes in the tercet, *The Prefiguration* and *Lumen Gloriae*, as quickly as I could, lucking into a copy of the first at a used bookstore in Chicago but spending more money than I really had at the time on the other. No matter—the books were necessary to have and their value magnified in my possession. (I gave all three to my brother when I found a pristine hardcover set of the *Trilogy* on the shelves at Woodland Pattern Book Center in Milwaukee for sale at cover price. "Lucky" insufficiently describes how I felt at that moment.)

Though the work in the *Trilogy* tends toward spareness and austerity, it's nevertheless suffused with the value of literary friendship. Samperi, typically described in biographical material as an orphan and auto-didact, came to poetry relatively early and had the fortune in 1957 to connect to Louis Zukofsky, who provided him tutelage as well as connections to a larger literary world. Most importantly, Zukofsky introduced Samperi to Cid Corman, who was living in Kyoto where he was publishing his literary magazine, *Origin*. Samperi was a fixture in *Origin*'s Second Series (1961–64), appearing regularly in the magazine, at times as a featured poet, and published alongside poets and artists such as Robert Kelly, Will Petersen, Lorine Niedecker, and Clayton Eshleman. When Samperi himself moved to Kyoto in 1964 to teach English, literary friendships with Corman, Petersen, and Eshleman, who were all also living there at the time, were soldered. Each would go on to be a supporter and publisher of Samperi's work, connecting him to a vibrant strain of the American Objectivist tradition active at the time in Japan.

Pulling all these connections together, in 1971, Mushinsha/Grossman, a press with whom Corman had significant influence (and who was publishing some of his own books at the time as well) issued *The Prefiguration*. In 1973, the other two books of the trilogy, *Quadrifariam* and *Lumen Gloriae* were issued. The titles of these three books give powerful clues to the work contained within the covers. A prefiguration is a foreshadowing of a person or a thing to come. It functions in Christian thought as a metaphorical anticipation in scripture, usually in the form of typology, a strategy of scriptural interpretation in which older realities, or types, are seen to foreshadow future realities, or antitypes, all according to God's plan of salvation. For instance, Moses is seen as the type for which Christ is antitype. Analogously, the human imagination on earth can be seen to anticipate the heavenly imagination. When Samperi writes,

> a beginning of snow
> and in a garden
> in moonlight
> an angel
>
> inwardly radiating

we can take this as both a heavenly premonition spied here in the earthly realm but also as a momentary anticipation of the work to come in his own imagination, for which "inwardly radiating" is an apt prefiguration.

Quadrifariam is a term drawn from a more peculiar source. It's a Latin adverb meaning "fourfold," which Samperi uses to refer specifically to Dante's four-tiered interpretive approach to scripture, which the poet himself drew from his readings of Saints Aquinas and Augustine. In Dante's letter to his patron Can Grande, he describes how scripture can be understood polysemously (a word Dante coined) on the literal, the allegorical, the moral (or tropological), and the anagogical (or mystical) levels. Furthermore, in the same letter, Dante informs Can Grande that his *Commedia* also operates using a three-fold pattern in its form, from the three canticles of *Inferno*, *Purgatorio*, and *Paradiso*, to the individual cantos in each part, down to the rhymed, musical tercets. In the note on the dust-jacket to *Quadrifariam*, Samperi mysteriously distils this to say, "The relationship bears a single experience, *One of the Intelligences*, that is, at one end implied (*The Prefiguration*), at the other established (*Quadrifariam*), therefore, the emotion *companionship*: however, *Quadrifariam* carries with it the descent, *book*, *canzone*, *song*, that is, *Eternity*, *Image*, *Gift*, which is to say that the collapse gets defined in a more detailed manner…" Imagine, then, placed atop the four-fold pattern of discernment a triune pattern of poetic intention, which, when turned like a geometrically shaped dial, generates a kaleidoscope of patterns that becomes the work itself.

Lumen Gloriae completes the theological propositions of Samperi's *Trilogy*. The phrase translates as "the light of glory" and refers to the transfigured light in creation that flashes into the mind perfecting it momentarily and giving it a glimpse of eternity. Appropriately, it's a much shorter book than the other two, made up of vivid flashes that confer the sense not so much of a spiritual attainment as a conviction in its invariable arrival:

> the more
> distant
> the wood
> the river
> the valley
> the more
> encompassing
> the bird
> spiraling

Re-reading the *Trilogy*, especially now that the three books have been republished in a single edition, a question arises. What is the novum in this work? Where does the new energy arise from? Those of us attracted to Samperi's poetry have tended to answer this question in terms of its spiritual import: this is a religious poetry of a Catholic, mystical strain, something at the time it was written very rare in American poetry and therefore in and of itself valuable. But I think a more specific innovation is at work in this poetry, one demonstrated in the three books' progressively developed convictions about the necessity of witnessing the passage of angels through the world. As they move through the world, these angels form vortexes, out from which the creative imagination emerges. There's a ghostly, morbid, and melancholic mood that suffuses the *Trilogy*, which begins, after all, with a fantasy of the poet's demise:

> On the night of my death
> fires will lace
> the shoreline
> of some unknown beach—

Another poem in *The Prefiguration* begins with the line, "a phase a despair." A struggle against acedia pervades the earlier poems in this volume with poetic efforts to resist the spiritual torpor life in the alienating city encourages in a lonely wanderer. The feeling in the work shifts perceptibly in "Morning and Evening," largely a prose meditation that begins, "A man going away to sorrow." Sorrow as a verb but also a place. The man walks through a world of shadow and dusk, through city streets and parks, included in the world as a witness but disconnected from it. He talks to himself, he breaks into Scholastic Latin, he looks for the glorified body, he notices shabby details and beautiful flashes. Along the way, he ciphers an angel's movements: "Concerning an angel dying by a river and a man sorrowing in a street and the nature of the prefiguration of the one of the other depending upon whether one's by a river or in a street." This mirroring amplifies "Foreknowledge's fault" as well as providing a way to write about the inwardly radiating angel he notices in the moonlight. By the time he's completed the passage through this valley of darkness, his writing has changed. The poems become more crystalline but stranger. There's an incredible confidence to the verse but also a rhythm and prosody not always immediately apprehensible. "Crystals," the collection in *The Prefiguration* immediately following "Morning and Evening," begins with one of Samperi's boldest claims: "The new man is always the spiritual man."

The luminous core of the *Trilogy* for me is "The Triune," the work that begins *Quadrifariam*. This is a sequence of forty-four untitled poems, each thirty-five lines long running the length of the oblong page and for which there is no obvious precedent in American verse. At one glance, they appear to be Objectivist lists; at another, dazzling theological abstractions; at another, a series of threshold crossings, from city to park, from sadness to gladness. Following a suggestion by poet John Martone (another publisher, editor, and friend of Samperi's), I like to regard these poems as stations of the cross, recorded on a via dolorosa from which glimpses of the light of glory might be caught. "I walked conversing with angels," the sequence begins, never relenting from that proposition. In these poems, the angelic knowledge intuited in "Morning and Evening" descends into three-fold structure—you feel the book, the canzone, and the song settling into place. If I were to pick a poem in this sequence that resonates most harmonically with the *Trilogy* as a whole, I would choose the thirty-eighth in which Eternity, Image, and Gift begin to collocate in the poem's mystical, anagogical potentials. It begins,

> Spirit the spirit an identification
> water an image significantly subject
> the revelation the man
> resolution the projection
> the man another an extension the one below
> If point no boundary
> then point invalid
> metaphorical
> the man reference
> the universe creation
> eternity
> image
> use

Some of the unusual features of Samperi's verse-making are visible here, especially his lack of punctuation and his emphatic prosody. You might call this poetry abstract but I'm always impressed by the way Samperi takes abstract nouns (*identification* and *revelation*, for instance) and uses them as concrete particulars, as visible portions of the world or the man. The poem concludes,

> however
> differential
> integral
> appetitive
> the noetic
> self
> return
> pilgrimage image eternity

The image of eternity is pilgrimage, striving toward holiness, just as the word "image" is nested inside "pilgrimage."

In the middle of this poem, we find the lines, "fire / plain / angel / visional." Samperi's invocation of angels, I've come to find, is incredibly sophisticated, visionary and apocalyptic, even as it is plainly matter of fact, something the poet sees as he takes his walks. Saint Augustine, in *The City of God*, writes, "God speaks not in a bodily but a spiritual voice, not to sense but to understanding, not in words dwelling in time, but, if I may say so, eternally, neither beginning to speak not coming to the end of speech. And the angels, who have been eternally blessed in enjoying God's incommunicable truth to the full, hear God in a more complete way. They hear the message of their ministry not with the body but with the mental ears."[2] Attentive to angelic intercession, Samperi seeks to hear God in a more complete way. In this sense, his work performs a valuable apocalyptic, which is to say revelatory, function. Traditionally, in Jewish and Christian tradition, there are two forms of apocalyptic narrative. In one, a seer is taken on a fantastic, celestial journey in which cosmological secrets are revealed. In another, there is no such journey. Instead, the writing broods on the meaning of history and its imminent end. Samperi's *Trilogy* combines these into a luminous dialogue with the heavenly, in which the morose state of the mundane is revealed to hide lodes of glorious light made visible and audible by traversing the world with eyes and ears informed by angelic knowledge. "I lived daily the spiritual," he writes in one poem. More high-mindedly, in another, he intones (I imagine these lines uttered in trance-like ecstasy):

> the glorified body the individual the universe
> the identification the individual the universal formal
> individual universal an identification undefined
> *Spirit the spirit an identification*

It's the poetry, after all, that matters most. Its binding energies and its unleashed imagination. There's much here to fuel future poetry, future thought. In the *Trilogy*, we find Samperi mastering his art even as he wrestles— agonized and admirable— with its meanings.

—Peter O'Leary

---

2. Saint Augustine, *The City of God* X:15, in *Angelic Spirituality*, translated and introduced by Steven Chase, Classics of Western Spirituality (New York: Paulist Press, 2002), p. 85.

The Prefiguration

Contents

Song Book
7

Of Light
49

Branches
95

Ferns
121

Morning and Evening
131

Crystals
187

So Close
209

Song Book

On the night of my death
fires will lace
the shoreline
of some unknown beach—

and children
             in loose
                       half-length
            blue gowns
will sing my dirge
as unknown vagrants
place my body
on a raft
            covered with lilies
            and seaweed—

and after they have
fastened down my body
with rope
            they (the vagrants)
and the children
will set
                           the raft
        adrift

I am an anchorite.
   and (I am Manfred's half-brother.)

In the morning
I go to a coffee shop.

  Sunlight is
  on things.

the young wives are wheeling baby carriages
the old wives are carrying large packages of food

  The Avenue
  Seethes with health.

After I have had
My coffee and toast
I go back to my furnished room.

  I am stirred by some
  white blossoms near
  low uncut hedges.
  and

the wind cools my eyes—
for the trees are blinding.

In a moment
I shall be in the room
and I shall be glad.

  I cannot bear
  sunlight in the morning.

Some boys are talking
softly under a tree.
Some girls are sitting
on the stoop
of a two story stucco home.
They are hoping the boys will come over.

I pass them. I have had my supper.
I feel better at night.
The streets are less cruel.

I am in
the room again.
I am going
to hear Gieseking
Play Brahms'
Intermezzi.
              Then
I shall read
some of Landor's Conversations.

the trains

My room shakes.

                        run

I am lying on
my back in bed.

                        every

The lights are out.

                        five

Between the second and third finger
a lit cigarette hisses.

                        minutes

Anemone.

                        the

I think of anemones.

                        subway

And sequins. And reeds. And mice.

                        is

My deadness is now complete.

two blocks from
my room

I waste

        my afternoons
        in streets

where faces

        drift

in sunlight

        and brick homes

fling

        Mozart tunes

against Pet shops.

        Damn it,

There's something

        wrong

with this place,

        says an old man,

as I wait for a bus.

Memory
sends me
back

    time
     is
dread

       formerly,
the dead
moved
on the graveled path
past the chipped virgin

              and

children
      gathered
apples from
the nearby orchard

           green   and
           red

eyes caught
in the incense
going up

     and corn
     fields

burned

    up   and little boys stood
       at the fence watching

with sunlight

      and then went
      through a hole
      in the fence
      down to the farms

The sorrel
horses gallop
along a
dirt road

fields
recede

hills
flatten

cities
sink

—and the sorrel
horses
      continue
to gallop
      along the
moving dirt road.

Come here, by this window—look,
Up there, the sun has become inconstant.

    Hapless, I shall take
my little bag of necessities and move closer
toward the ivory gate—
       for I have paid
my debts, and having neither father nor
mother nor brother nor sister, I am now granted
freedom—which is the quickest way to death.
But I swear I shall die happy.

        To be saved I must
slip away from the moderns
                      quietly
and go to that land
I have heard
        so much
        about (the north wind
the gardens
full
with my favorite
lilacs.

There is no
sunlight
in this
room.
      Outside
the bee song
of people
and cars
      penetrates
this tomb
      of coldness
of darkness—

But
the features
the par
tic
u
lar i ties of
      the living
are not seen
by the Prince (
inmate
solitary
of this tower
without
windows).

Tune comes
from

the street:

dark, cold
treeless—

a cops' band

pactices in
the basement

of the apartment
house

near the car lot:

streetlight
opposite

the basement

lights
upon

the instruments
through

the open window—
stones,

glints
tangle—

free

as mind,
as fog.

Turn
look!

the brindled
west

lion

is stalking
the river-bank.

say goodbye;
greet owl, yes!

or, if you can,
at the high wall

ape Buddha.

An iron fence
a brick house—

blackbirds
in grass

at the edge
of the walk—

from
the ground floor

piano

base
treble—

toward
the back

in his garden
an old man

stooping

plants
seeds

heard from
the kitchen window.

A crowd
stood

in front
of

the church
gap-

ing as
four

pallbear-
ers

carried
the

coffin
down

the steps
to

the hearse
as

the grieved
chil-

dren of
the

deceased
were

singly
es-

corted
to

the fam-
i-

ly car—

after
when

the last
car

was seen
slow-

ly turn-
ing

around
the

corner
they

went their
way.

Among
rocks

looking down
on nude bathers

gulls high
against sky

gulls low
against high

ships
against

blackness

Window
looks

out on
the shore

rowboat
drifts

in toward
the bell buoy

water
infolds

comes up
goes back

rain
beginning

the winow
looks

and sees

eight birds
fly

down from
a tree

to drink
rain

water
from

the gutter

later—
two

spot
some crumbs

under
a car

five
scatter

as
children

run by
and

one flies
up

to a
window ledge

To give these words to someone,
   Wherein being shall be made known.—
   "No, my friend, no, I cannot hope

To get away. What you say, I know.
   I have always wanted new sights—
   Such as, the movement of a leaf

Struggling to free itself from a branch.
   But I also know that if free I shall fall.
   So I stay with my books, and sometimes make songs.

It is better, I mean, to be here,
   Where the mind can act
   And make light where there is none,

Than with the crowd, whose mouth defies the sun.
   No I can never go; it is dark beyond my gate;
   And my mind could not live out there."

I shall go where light is clean
(this, too, I know is inapposite
to a way);
nevertheless

emerge
and gain a
sight
of clear ground

from which one may—
as before he
couldn't
when

a wall
which admits
no light
but sound

secured him from,
as it were,
grossnesses
and, also,

possibly,
graces—

start again

and see
with eyes made clean
by an apt use

a haze
over
rich fields

and a hedge
alive.

Altho there is no evidence
in the streets,
hills, etc.,

that He exists

it is right to think
of Him to *be*:

viz.,
as a *conceptual limit*,
wherein order might be dreamed—

for an adept
once said:

the angles of
a given triangle

are equal to
two right angles

this I understand;
however, I'm not convinced
that such a triangle
exists—

where?—in nature,
of course—

where existence
can be gainsaid?—

yes—then, it's the mind
that gives a thing being?

yes   &
no.

A grotto
   A wonder
Of workmanship

Where a bird
   On the shoulder
Of a saint

Sings
   Of a night's
Calvary.

If prescient then knowing
of Its beginning is with Him,
if beginning can be
applied to It—

since even before the battle
He knew of It:
being that Is—

and since good, therefore, It couldn't *be* from Him:
but, maybe, It *is* with Him as His "I Am Not".

The Christ of meadows,
lost, prayerfully
awaits
a sunrise.

And the satyrs' lithe
movements tempt
the candor
of his aliveness.

I have seen him
in the garden
when a songbird
flew among bright
branches and a dog
barked in the street,
walk by a rose bush
and along a path of tulips
toward her grave,
which lies to the right
of an apple-tree,
and place a wreath
of white carnations
on the headstone.

This I have seen
him do many times.

My songs
would

praise
her doves;

but now shadows
pass

over
a wall—

and the broken
head

of a Cupid

lies
beside

a cobbled
walk

past
a hothouse.

Ice floes
  out
beyond
  wreckage

break
  against
a faint
  sunrise:

seabirds
  tumble
under
  a cliff

and bridal
  wreaths
mingle
  with rue.

Our
vines
burn
on

the
garden
wall—
also,

snow
lightly
covers
the

shovel
by
the
wooden

steps.

Of Light

daybreak—

chicks
under
the
wing

nightfall—

a
dimming
of
trees

How long I've leaned against the screen-door!
Our porch empty of the few guests we've ever had;
And the white roses, under the shadeless window
That looks toward the freight yard—dead, too.

You say
　I'm not:
so trees
　bloom?

tired,
　I gave
love, sat
　on grass—

held
　your head
up; even
　a cop

thought
　it new
that a
　lover's

eyes
　could be
bloodshot:
　wakeful,

I knew
　only
a dawn
—and you.

Cavalcando l'altr'ier per un cammino

Riding the other day along a road,
   thoughtful of this hateful journey,
   I found Love up a ways in shadows
   in the tattered clothes of a pilgrim.
   He seemed wretched
   as if he'd lost lordship;
   and he came sighing, with head bowed
   —I guess, not to see people.
When he saw me, he called out,
   and said: "I come from a far place,
   where by my power your heart was—
   now I bear it to serve a new pleasure."
   Then I took in effect his movements,
   and he vanished, but how I cannot say.

                    this thinking
can't overreach
body
nor body
thinking:

            seeming one,
we're music's
nightly
spell
—not spheres'.

Tonight I, hero, have drunk wine—
For no doves tremble above the golden branch.
Now I stumble along a low garden wall;
And pray I'll soon fall toward hidden grass.

I will take away the hedge
and it shall be wasted—
the lovers placed

a long table
on the
lawn

and crowded
it with
meats, wine-bottles

and clusters
of grapes—
later

they walked
naked
among the

panthers
crouched in
the trees'

shadows.

The roses, song, droop
        On the trellis;
  Dried petals, shadows
Are this garden's music.

    a dream
      a falling away
      into darkness

    after wandering thru
      the wood
      coming out

    standing on the edge
      looking down
      the slope

    the church
      to the right
      behind pine trees

    the playground
      to the left
      behind the school

    slanting up
      more pine tree
      on top

    arranged in rows
      against the sky
      behind the fence

came down
　to a river
sat under a willow

birds flew
　from the river-bank
over the wood's treetops

to mountains

The garden's
fig tree's
covered
with burlap

and the leaves
on the grass
are wet
with rain—

nor yet has
the twittering
of a bird
on a hillside

waked me
to the glint
of grass
at the gate.

...must
you talk

of failure;

even this
snow's

right

—ah, oak,
branching

over
my work

shed

a phase a despair
in hope or dying
worrying least
whether the voice

behind the screen's
more like faith
or undivided
—or why ivy vines

after snow
forsythia
bloom against
a white fence

no luck left
only
a memory
of a child

behind
his
attic
window

Come
scatter
the garden's
bloosoms

on the hill
above
the beach!
an old man

under
an umbrella
lies toward
water

where a ship
sails out
beyond
a cliff.

in memory

the old
men stand
outside
the fence

near the
grape arbor
of the small
two family

house

Not soul, but body
  otherwise limping we go;
  Intelligences' substance

tautologic;
  matters not, really,
  glass vase

and liquid in it
  that seems
    same color—

An old lady
    behind
some artificial
  flowers looks

from her dirty
    ground
floor window
  at the kids

in the school
    yard
a block up
  from the

repair shop
    for the
city's
  buses.

Taking
the train
back to
Brooklyn—

thinking
always day
posits
your intent

in the
renewing
as in
the old—

my loneliness
greets
a friendly
world

even
the painted
sign
on a factory

wall:
House
of the
Dairymaid.

    Nothing so good
as this thought
of green under light
wherein branch

    over branch against
sun moves toward
its green under
a guise of light

Icicles
hang

from
branches

glass
under

branches
sun

glass
sun

icicles
icicles

falling

down past
rocks
children
running

under
leaves
beyond the
bench

fronting
grass
where birds
hover

against
the trees
in back-
ground

relieved
here and
there by
apartments

because
of the
steps
leading

up
to
the
street

   in
      music's
least melody
  there's

a memory
    its beginning's
a flowering
  of light

At
   return
of
   memory—

when
   morning
light's
   behind

roofs—
   the first
sight's
   of roses

on the
   garden
gate—
   then:

fading
   shadows
of
   a dream.

below
levels
of
hills
white
horses
galloping
down
the
road
from
the
wood
above
the
valley
at
the
foot
of
the
range
of
mountains
in
moonlight
against
stars

up

beyond

mountains

a

grove

beneath

rays

of

light—

below:

eagles'

shadows

gliding

toward

valleys

    the

        garden's

    paths

        darken

    under

        plum

    blossoms

        in

    shadows

        from

    the

        walls

going out
　　to
　　　　the backyard
　　to shovel snow

　　away from
　　the
　　　　cellar door
　　an old man

　　looked up
　　at
　　　　a shadeless
　　window

　　blinding
　　in
　　　　the sun
　　setting

　　behind the
　　homes
　　　　　beyond
　　the freight yard

the

trains

shaking

the

dust

from

the

El

scatter

the

birds

from

the

trees

to

the

roofs

a

branch

in

bloom

in

the

light

from

the

hills

trembles

under

the

lighting

of

birds

hills

behind

the

branches'

shadows

up

past

a

fountain

slope

toward

light

upward

in

    light

flame

in

flame

    dying

to

its

memory

    of

snow

this
quiet's
but

a
fall
of

light
from
hill

to
shore
where

the
odor
of

the
rose's
more

of
sea
than

earth

Branches

A wind's in the persimmon tree—
Come under its rustling.

And so
   the bird
was

said
   to rise
from

cinders—
   a way
of

holding
   the sun
to

heart.

Always
       now
for me
  in dreams—

yes!
       at noon,
too—
  children

in shade
       longing
for the
  grass

along the
       house
wall
  in light.

You see
tho
    leaves
fall

    the stars—

out at
all
    times
for

in
no
    time's
sake.

                        in memory
of your memory of a time far back:

                        birds
to your call falling to your
shoulders

Claudia,
Autumn's
come round
again—

now
leaves
like birds
tumble

from
the hill
behind
our

garden
overlooking
grass sloping
toward

sea.

looking
toward
the
wooded

hill
under
moonlight
you

spoke
of
the
rose

leaves
of
our
marriage

day

tho now it's only noon
    we speak of moonlight
on the trees among the houses
    closed in by the hills

in
  the
after
  rain

a
  child
stirs
  in

the
  wood
beyond
  the

clovers
  in
the
  tree's

shadow
  above
the
  moored

rowboats

If they knew
why this grief
the hour when
men gather in
fishing nets
or boy alone
on a hill
hesitates between
light and shadow
they wouldn't go
looking backward
along this river
below the olive grove.

To carry a song
into the city,
not to come away
with a prize—
this can't be
considering
in memory
the aftermath
of burntwood—
but nevertheless
to sing of a rose
against a sunrise
and of a man
moving toward water.

You're in light, song;
birds on branches
already in bloom
begin to twitter;
nighttime's behind you,
which, in truth, can
never enter into
the melody you have in heart:
see, the old men
sit above the river
twisting toward the ocean,
and the children
carrying baskets of lilac sprigs
turn momentarily
to look at the hills and woods
around the city.

from
the cold
wood
a silence
close
upon
a fluttering
of birds

beyond
behind the
apple-trees
among the
telephone
poles
on the
hillside
a falling
of

leaves

in the wind from the wood

a woman

stoops to gather

wild flowers

at a bridge

      No longer
the singing the melody
following upon the seeing
light from the hills
from the particles
either way
a way of getting beyond light's ghosts
but in the voicing
—no sun today
and a drunk shivering in a doorway—
a falling toward dream
or a wandering
among trees along
a river

      in love in longing
remembering a dream
of a cliff
crumbling away from under him
and the birds
beaten down by the storm
along the coastline
a man
walks in a meadow
casting least
shade
—Come sit
under a tree
in the shadow of the farthest hill;
there, before you
a river

and the flamingoes

The trees
along the road
up to the rocks
against the moon
loom above the dead
leaves

    Of the sea
coming to the imagination
under an aspect
of tar
comes to the mouth
after a night
spent at a window
looking toward the darkest
outline
of the highest hill
revealing fewest
stars

yesterday's
hills:
    birds,
insects—

today's:
wreckage
    under
light

    Passing by
a bridge
and then over the one
over the dried stream
to a field
along a wood
sloping toward rocks
above sea
a man
a woman
and a child

Ferns

Dolores,
now I make
my songs
for you—
I don't need
a window
at least
not the one
seeing you
and Claudia
as branch
over water
at the foot
of a hill
in morning
light

    You've

seen me

in pain

moonlight

on

my hands

my talk

dying

away

Today
we'll probably
go sit in the park
or maybe
on the bench
in front of
the bus stop
by the hospital
at least until
the sun goes
down

this crisis
of our life
when the stars
mean little

as background

Morning and Evening

A man going away to sorrow.

The furnished room: a bed a chair an end table and a lamp on it. Lo giorno se n'andava…: he lay dying.

Morning and no sun—neverthless wandering under a hill, a man looking toward rocks and so much farther down a wood.

Architectural pomposity: reflections of cars and pedestrians in the shop windows in the skyscrapers of maximum glass.

Sitting under light as if it were a tree, no shadow anywhere around him, a man who no longer remembers, seeing the whole world among branches.

With star and from star and from one's gathering of the

significance of each, a transformation whose flowering's a new heaven and a new earth.

From a hill, a man down from a hill, weary of solitude and the cold night, sees the waves against the sunrise and the gulls under the cliff.

To gather a spirit up out of its own consciousness: He stood at the foot of a hill and the flowers and animals around him gave off odors suggesting the perfection of fragrance beyond the hill. Walking slowly, passing by the stream to the left of a grove, the grass everywhere perfect in the morning light, some birds swift under branches, some lighting some hovering, he came to a place of roses and lilacs to the right of a grotto, and then past a willow climbed the fullness of path.

Continuing: If he was capable of seeing the phenomnality behind any impossibility of extrication, then to be in the dark and at peace was more of the nature of a forthcoming transfiguration.

One would have it illusion another fault and either may take offense at the other's sense of former and latter.

Concerning two lines opposite each other whose point in common (and equalizer) is perpendicular: the point in common (and equalizer) if infinitely removed would still remain the point in common (and equalizer).

Foreknowledge's fault: neither light nor darkness, and then light and darkness and the inclusion completing the one dispelling the other.

He wandered into an area of shops and bars: people hung about the corners—streetlights and neons dominated—no inkling of hope in the signs—if there were stars no reason to look up: a man could determine his direction by relation to mechanical light.

He walked along a shore and then up a path to a hill—dawn at the edge of grass.

Awake! and the hills remain. Sleep! and the awakening that is a dream sees the land sleeping in the folds of the horizon.—More snow on the ground—however, not so bad—the wind's died down.

He walked along the shops under the El—a few blocks down, the ocean.

At the foot of a slope, a man in the light from branches, sees clusters of birds in the glare above the hills.

Concerning an angel dying by a river and a man sorrowing in a street and the nature of the prefiguration of the one of the other depending upon whether one's by a river or in a street:

An angel came down a hill and moved among the flowers along the river-bank to a place where river and grass twisted toward deepest wood; then following more to the right than the line of the river he saw a white flower and a path. Sorrowing along the path, imagining flowering trees on a hillside and birds in the shadows of a grove, he moved as if downward, taking his sense from his movement down the hill, and came to a brook reflecting animals fleeing to woods and at the same time revealing as if under glass birds dying in a withered tree. Then going on, he passed under overhanging rocks to a meadow past vines. He kept close to shadow and a little ways down turned in on grass leading toward what seemed sea. In memory he saw a land exempt from the misery that placed the hill under the deepening of shadow. When he reached the roses at the foot of the slope what seemed sea was instead ice; then he took the path beyond the lilies: along the way, off behind the rocks in the weeds, a stirring of animals. After crossing a stream and climbing a hillock, he moved down into a valley. He felt as if he were at the edge of a field next to a forest in moonlight under sky sloping toward stars. Then he came to a path leading upward past mountain ledges looking down on land revealing to each level its horizon. Continuing along the path, seeing eagles swooping down on prey, remembering the grass gradually fading as he approached declivity, he moved into a grove where leaf and songbird trembled under faintest wind, and then down above branches growing out of cracks in rocks to a field in snow. Then he turned to the left and some ways up beyond the trees under the hill came to forsythia in bloom on a slope.

If a work is primarily addressed to God, then it follows that the audience isn't essential—in fact, a period that places the movement in the audience whose referential is the standard that impedes draws to itself a principle whose point is finally to exclude totally: therefore, it is right to say that no identifications can be telically intended when a work is so primarily addressed.

The other movement: We moved to another place—and what seemed to be direction of another sort was, in truth, only a second period devoid of a wake but nevertheless profound enough to transform memory.

"Do you think a writer needs a room of deepest darkness?"—"Yes!"—"Does deepest quiet mean darkness?"—"No!"—"Then why use the word deepest...."

"Is it possible to write amidst noise?"—"No doubt—a truism even speaks of a part inwardly contained."—"Yes! but If one contains himself even amidst noise, can the word be anything but dynamically scanned? that is, each to each discontinuously rooted?"—"To project no argument as answer would place the meaning in an implication whose release would be to draw to itself a view no longer implicative."

Conversations with oneself: they've a way of going on even in book shops where one goes only to browse—and then after satiety, one finds himself in a street ostentatiously structured toward the intellective that gathers in only for the sake of the river-god who demands that the flow continue—and the shops along the way are not an afterthought. From this it becomes valid to say that what is commonly called direct vision is, in truth, just that and no more, that is, the integument is the reflection; therefore, if you walk a street and come out with a presupposition that is a plain whose persective is homeric, then you are as they say in the world but not of it.

Given a beginning, it is true to say that by the second or third day a man's words falter—he falls away from that confrontation that makes him secure even tho each step shows him to others a man to be shunned.

There are those who are so sure of a place in letters that smugness is the upshot to the idiom nothing can displace them—this comes from a contemporaneity moving them to conceive of themselves as the originators of a movement whose touchstone is in proportion to the audience's relation to the referential wholly civil.

One can go on writing like this for a lifetime and still not be false to a movement opposed to a work in progress.

From Leibniz' "Car (quelque paradoxe que cela paraisse) il est impossible à nous d'avoir la connaissance des individus et de trouver le moyen de déterminer exactement l'individualité d'aucunne chose, à moins de la garder elle-même; car toutes les circonstances peuvent revenir; les plus petites différences nous sont insensibles; le lieu ou le temps, bien loin de déterminer d'eux-mêmes, ont besoin eux-mêmes d'etre déterminés par les choses qu'ils contiennent" the clearest insight is: state as unity as space and civil right as time; therefore, seen this way the differential calculus is progressive.

Deeper thought reveals a yes and no in the statement: propositions de fait propositions de raison.

Mind discouraged again—long walks as curative—hope this place causes me to move about differently each day.

There's a sorrow that arises from a contemplation unable to come to grips with a work that needs to complete itself and say: it's a new period and the time of fulfillment closer.

"Should a writer feel guilty that he makes no money from his work?"— "No!"—"Even if he makes no money another way?"—"If his work brings in no money, then he's in the same position as any other unemployed worker;

however, since it is granted that the audience substantiates his position as artist, it leaves him little hope of help from 'welfare'—therefore, he must let go of the one and take on the other, that is, poverty and not feel guilty."

Since civilization is not for the poor, there isn't much to it—by the poor one means the world before God; therefore, one obviates the condescending tone "does not include".

"…quod ideo est quia scientia habetur de rebus secundum quod sunt in sciente, voluntas autem comparatur ad res secundum quod sunt seipsis. Quia igitur omnia alia habent necessarium esse secundum quod sunt in Deo, non autem secundum quod sunt in seipsis, habent necessitatem absolutam, ita quod sint per seipsa necessaria; propter hoc Deus quaecumque scit ex necessitate; non autem quaecumque vult ex necessitate vult." When natural theology appropriates the above, we get an image of God as "mechanical wizard": that is the State has succeeded in drawing its variables unto itself.

"Can you honestly say that modern literature is beyond these traps that are societally 'formalized'?"—"It would seem that the most argute state propaganda is to imply the contrary in its use of its most intransigent subjects: that is, 'free society' conducive toward free literature, which is to say, each author is left more or less alone to satisfy the

audience occupying a mean reflective position, which the 'lone author' conceives as his to mould by astonishment, taking his sense to act from 'free society' granting him this illusion to discover, thereby giving ample praise to a progressiveness, whose Unitary Field Theory is discontinuous, therefore, circular, and whose image is shoreline to sea...."
—"Can you tell us anything about merit?"—"Yes! it doesn't work here."

"Unde perfectio naturae angelicae requirit multiplicationem specierum, non autem multiplicationem individuarum in una specie."

Modern criticism views let us say a 16th century poet and proceeds to divest him of an 18th century critic's view, never owning up to it—else why criticism at all—that the next century stands to rid him of his slant. There's something ad infinitum about this.

It seems that I haven't said what I've wanted to say, that is, when confronted by such a tradition—and yet the idea is not opposed to tradition—no reason to write seems to be the honest action, that is, of course, if we accept audience as end, but since God is the reason we write, then it follows that the perspective that is historical is pointless.

Little relation to the civil: does this make me uncivil?

"Isn't it a pity that in the end an artist becomes just

another example of grandiose state propaganda!"—"Yes! but even more piteous is the image of his youth."

It is better not to know what I've written yesterday—not that one writes to discard, but when there's a sense that I'm not right today, then the next day leaves me in the position of a viewer of things under the hill; therefore, it is fair to say: I have no world.

Everything down here just teems with the give and take that is exploitative.

To take up what was said above: if one continued to write as if the right hand were unaware of the left, then at the completion of such a work he could only be as much surprised as any possible reader. But the sorrow that arises from such a writing can only be compared to a journey unaware of every step along the way but the end in mind fully presupposed and, of course, the reason for moving. This end in mind should be solace, but somehow, because of the steps along the way, it leaves the sorrowing man ever in a state of renewal or better vigilant enough to know that if tense then bowed, if relaxed, that is suggestive of flesh bespeaking least or more truly no bone, then bleassed, full of the peace that gets you thru, that is, least or again more truly no trace of the other world, that is, circle, passed thru.

One wishes to write honestly: therefore, is it honestly to

be concerned primarily with the rhythm of language? isn't the triumph in the very vanquishing of language?—Don't be misled: language is your better part, and the flow is life. —If language is the better part, then since you call the flow life, it follows that language is to matter as the flow is to soul, which is to say, if so, then the flow is a consequence of the matter language....—Logic is circular: is the angelic nature circular?

Again: light and darkness—if evil is a privation of the good, then evil is not an opposite: does this make the good tautologic?

"When you pose a statement in the form of a question, have you already answered it?"—"Yes! but it seeks to enlist another—this establishes it as an argument, altho the calm to be revealed makes it ever singular."

"There's always so much more going on—a writer could draw completely only haphazardly—you it seems place yourself—it's criticism; I do it not to hurt, but to make you, eventually, of course, realize yourself more in the way that is cultural—in a position too inward; therefore, you force the reader to bow his head—this kind of art is at least from the historical view immature and altogether misleading: it uses simple words and expects us to come up with an even greater simplicity and yet at the same time gives also indirectly the involvements that are of greatest complexity—you cannot expect a people inured to surface to accept your depth."

No one, of course, speaks to me in the words of the above; therefore, why not give myself over to such words! they place me in direct relation to my daily walks—people move I move—rapidly: is the street the river? the sidewalks its banks? buildings a wood's tallest trees? is a man insane to see distortion of this sort? or is it really the builder who in the withdrawal from "the natural whose presupposition is creation" impedes the will only to make it take stock, that is, unlearn the learning, come finally to the glory that laid no traps?

Should mention that the works meant as criticism ended up in praise of...: can such a writing be valid?

The gloom reaches down—a valley a prey to deepest shadow: what's above?

Lovely birds my birds singing in the backyards of stone and rubble—

So many windows from the ground floor to the 5th facing the row of tenements opposite, and each to each immutable except for the snap of shade the fall of light and the abysmal yawning gap the backyard.

window sill in light

　　blind

　　branch bird
　　shadow

　　radio

Light altering things—angelic nature in time and not time that is planetary, but rather time that measures virtually —what kind of time is that? is it cosmic time? out of a man's reach?—Read of angelic power! its movement that can be either continuous or discontinuous—is the discontinuous its better movement? and yet either movement in no way to be compared to "things corporeal in movement"—does it leave you guessing? science distorting an ancient definition —taking unto itself for the sake of the more intense or better world-wide slavery—should a man damn science? or rather see it rightly, that is, that which is for sole consideration of truth—is truth outside? more complex than in head? therefore, why consideration of motion? and the other aspect of science, that is, the more prudential whose impediment is use-value as substance (and this not to say that the other side's any better—in fact, in a way even worse—

feigning a system conducive toward free movements)....
You've again written indirectly—and yet you've been direct in the way that abstracts from here and now: thus another inverse ratio.

A man in deep darkness hears birds and imagines flowers.

Let there be words to express a child's gaze at moon: in father's arms, she points at the moon and says: bird! not knowing the moon's name—then hearing its name, she delights in it—says it over and over—they pass the shops, the avenue busy as ever; and then at a corner father sees the moon just a little to the side of an apartment building—he reminds; child says over and over: moon moon...: sleep my child heavenly under moon!

What constitutes a true definition of sentimentalism? a risk involving a man in a past whose ambience is sensible? should an angel look down upon a man? God forbid!

"You must not let them get you down—whatever they say, it's beside the point: that is, their ultimate interest is how much is in it for them; therefore, to subsidize you would be false to an age checking every gift to see how much is risk how much is to their advantage (that is, 'the force behind', which leads upward to munificent capitalist, who in turn draws us completely to participate in the choral praise of the Material Ideal, the State)."—"When you use the word

choral, are you thinking of it anteriorly? I mean, the dance?"
—It is now late afternoon: hear paraphrastic words: How do I know? the Father has told me.

Writing of misery and in the long run isolated from the world, a man can only move along streets as if no relation were possible. Yesterday, for instance, everything went wrong, and so he thought of streets, but once out and amidst the flow things fell away or began to topple—so he was left alone in a plain—of course, he knew that this was illusion; but again, he thought what is the cause of this illusion: "The only cure for your malaise is manual labor—you should stop your wandering, feeling as if the world were in distance—your logic is leading you astray; therefore, work hard—forgot the inwardness—the great thing about our century is just this: we've succeeded in getting everybody into the hard labor market—and it's good—it keeps the inward ones from going off on pilgrimages. You must not see this as an error, rather you should—using all your strength—come to its feast—it doesn't exclude; in fact, it wants you and your children. I repeat: give yourself to physical labor—what you do is not labor—it can't be measured." There's movement in air but it isn't light.

I've returned from another long walk—the day so depressing, but, of course, it isn't the day, it's the sorrow so deeply inward—and maybe to use depth is still to be in perspective—a reason why there's something frustrating about that direction, too.

One involved in a way foreign to anterior and posterior must consider it true that work done "isn't looked back to" for a different reason.

Angelic knowledge despite "species connatural" is still a confrontation.

There can be no audience when a work's vision is total. Since the final pleasure is the whole work in mind, then "in the end" implying only "some statements" does not hold.

The park was crowded today—no reason to stay away—but always why parks built within city rather than cities within park—not right to pose this even as a question let alone become sorrowful over it—but nevertheless you find yourself being drawn to them—yes! to take a breather—and the best reason for being there is the child.

Then there is the movement away from the park: along the streets is the direction, and the sense is supposedly straight—this illusion adds to the sentiment "my city". No man can escape this trap—for by extension the suburbs and deserts are but the city in extension. So you continue to walk, and every relation comes to you insincerely.

Now you think of various religious and sciences—and when seen from the standpoint of the city, an image of the world belaboring an issue never to be at rest, and the stress is just that, that is, the encomium to commotional world, and the city the better for it, teaching the citizens no life only burden of death, reduces the mind to stoical severity as its only triumph over quotidian movement.

You have your work—no amount of impediment can hold you back—you must if need be think that each word is in praise of the Word—it comes to that! give yourself up to Him and then place is yours or better is of no account for just that reason of love.

The world has its own, therefore, it seeks to establish the Christ-Phenomenon as the outcome of the Graeco-Roman Hebraic clash—this makes it cultural; therefore, those who labor for a new culture are justified in their desire to exculpate themselves from any action that deracinates: that is, they wish the crime to be enacted by the masses. Antichrist cannot triumph, for the life has nothing to do with progress as such, that is, the conservative and liberal dependent upon the so-called infinite straight line—nor is tradition of any concern, nor does this mean that restatement is necessary.

You must come to grips again with the principle of

individuation: the difference is formal the singular material —the singular cannot be known in itself because intelligence is spiritual, therefore, it is by way of abstraction that the singular is known simpler than it is; however, species intellectus angeli, quae sunt quaedam derivativae similitudines a divina essential, sunt similitudines rerum, non solum quantum ad formam, sed etiam quantum ad materiam.

It now seems valid to see man's relation to the Gift, that is, the image of a man at the foot of a hill, revealing the angels similarly disposed—the signification of this revelation shows up the fault of pantheism.

When it is said that the angels behold God's wisdom, the meaning is: dwelling in His City; but when it is said that they do not comprehend it, then the heart obviates: are they at rest in it? establishing a kind of trust holding even them in check—God's wisdom completely informs them, holds back nothing that is theirs; therefore, no tragic ache can subsist in them.—"How do you explain the Fall?"—"How do you explain Salvation?"

It might be mentioned here: if a man in stressing the angels' inability to comprehend the Divine Wisdom states nevertheless it isn't necessary to know everything in it, then he says in effect the same that was said above.

The morning and evening knowledge of the angels is a

refinement of the principle of individuation: that is, to know things in God and things in themselves is to know angelically. (It should be mentioned again: the principle of individuation does away with the knowledge of things in themselves.) When it was said above that "the singular cannot be known in itself because intelligence is spiritual", it was done more to state the implication, intelligence, rather than that "the singular cannot be known in itself because of the matter".

Aquinas has treated Aristotle and Plato justly by quelling all talk concerning tabula rasa and innate ideas.

A good morning walk! cloudy at first, therefore, streets almost deserted—then after a pause at a book store, started again to walk—this time to a park—sun out, therefore, streets becoming crowded—in the park, the various kinds of people, more various because of the outfits rather than "the head structure, the skin"—therefore, words come to mind: why then argument running out *race race*!—sitting down, letting the child play—two girls playing catch in the distance—coming closer to move the child to join them—child responds immediately! before that: lady walking dog responds to child because child shows no fear of dog—lady moves away—girls take unto themselves the whole movement—beyond: the fountain and around it the various kinds—ball remains in a puddle—child moves away—girls who remain also as fixed as ball nevertheless fall away—then the walk continues along streets lined with paintings—child sees the ones representing birds various animals—there is the clash between the bright ones and the somber ones: the sun shines forth! finally out if it—now only shops to see—just before turning up a street heading toward home, a playground: groups gathered here and there along its fence: sun now noon!

To a man whose shoes are falling apart a movement toward a park is a movement toward unearthly existence.

He came to a park and then after some searching for a place to sit to a bench as if that time were without reference to another time far back or up head...

Neither to sow nor to reap—

It is important that you let go none of your principles—

Songs tonight may get you thru the night better than drink—

But the angels are being reduced to the clever atomic theory—

Fly up and then out unto areas of transformation—

Let the mind awaken in the way a man opens a door to a hallway of darkness and feculence and still senses the odor of lilacs—

To be in the way implies no end because the beginning is no longer implicative—

None of this will get you anywhere, altho you can go on indefinitely—

A drunk all bloody upsets the balance of commercial movement—no one cares—if he were to drop dead in an alley, they'd leave him and say the better place, but the law requires that a truck come to cart him off to immemorial ground—"life goes on"; no man can stop to give thought to a drunk all bloody.

"Give us another form rather than that old reform, and you'd see no Skid Row—"

"You'd see fields and no notion of surplus could arise from them—"

See the drunks sitting at the windows above the restaurant—

See the drunks unable to get up—

Legless men selling shoe laces—

But they have nothing to sell—they're simply unable to get up off the street—

Wounded animals! the pedestrians see no more than images of animals—

Sorrowful animals! bloody animals! dragging their broken, dispirited bodies thru forests—

No traffic has concern for them—
No charitable organization is truthful enough—
No longer face to face charity—rather relegation to institution bent on screening applicants—
Traffic continues—
Shop owners stand outside shops—
They pose—
Cigar their sign of success—
Policemen stand at corners—
Shop owners and policemen greet each other—
Legless drunk finally drags himself into an alley—
Traffic triumphs—
To stress even this aspect of city is to say it incorrectly, that is, the others use similar tactics—if you're against a race then the best way to write against it is: raise scatologic news up front! that is, single out and let mob carry out sentence universally.
My beloved's lost in Babylon—
My beloved nevertheless sings of the waters of Babylon—
My son, the beloved, is a shepherd to none of the people because none know my son, the beloved—
My beloved son gather up my lost people—
My son, the beloved, is a shepherd to all of the people because all know my son, the beloved—

And then there is the East—which one comes off best?—pit them against one another—see both as outcomes of clashes, therefore, of little importance except as Types

None of this makes sense! East as Beginning West as End—East and West opposites

Not to the Sun!

A man awakens early to go down to the freight yards—

A man awakens from *that* awakening to know that the level is street—

A man falls down in the street—

Rain—

Litany is invalid too because it presupposes an audience equally interested in the same object of adoration as the speaker.

Walk downtown—go to areas of renovation—think upon the meaning of a structure built *with a look toward the horizon.*—But what about the meaning of tall buildings confronting you with a closeness that is almost natural?—See it as a lie!—Yes! every lie misleads you. What is right architecture?—One thing is sure: it is not nature presupposed by motion.

Every statement that you make if it releases you from a notion that is dialogic alters the ostensible dialog in a movement ultimately concerned with the Light that Is and the light that is by participation.

"To write as if every substantive were not valid unless first adjectivally qualified—this presupposition's behind even the most austere work: therefore, do you mean to imply that your work is not so founded?"—"Yes!"—"Then you must be saying something other than what the work conveys."—"You seem to be criticizing yourself—not me."

Children in a garden—

Waiting to catch a train, a man thinks back, oblivious to the empty station and the hills behind it—

Children in a street—

A man walks the whole city without a cent in his pocket—

Cents in this city are dollars in another—

What next: children up from a wood come down a hill—

Like what?—

Like shadow—

Birds fly up as children run down—

You'll have to go for blocks before you see a tree in this city—

…then you walk along warehouses till you come to the tallest building—you turn right and some two or three blocks up you'll find a park….

"The nature of city speech: to keep you moving: up

and down."—"I don't think you're using the word nature correctly."—"I get your meaning—birth is different from purpose."

An experiment: go to a park—sit on a bench and listen—then go home and try to write the variety of voices: you can't do it—no man can—you're always trying to make it simpler than it is: that's the reason why no man is capable of banning works of art.

Necessary question: then how is it possible that city structure impedes the will?

What is the nature of grief?—To see a man who belongs to no city is to see grief; however, to be in the world but not of it is his way to Life.

If you spent your whole day trying to find reasons why you should love God and man, then you'd be in the very predicament that is against nature.

It seems that images of poverty can be used only for the sake of propaganda, that is, the end involved is the State paternally concerned for its whole household: so the wonder is: how can the State act paternally?

Again the contradiction is: seeing the city from the top floor of the highest building, and then later on, seeing a drunk dying in a doorway.

Passing by a home for the aged, you see the old people

grouped under beach umbrellas, and the flowers and grass seem immobile.

You've reached a depth of despair from which no gathering up is possible: to wander is to have little voice to interest others—in a place of depth, the cry to a world above reaches never so high but only returns back revealing you even deeper than before—but there's an end to this depth, this you repeat to yourself as you go down even lower than the depth occurring from the cry returning.

Given a notion of blessedness, how much more salutary is the grace whereby blessedness is merited. But once blessedness is attained no notion of merit is compatible with it—charity completes itself, seeing fully.

Nothing that is natural shall be done away with, but the perfection that comes from blessedness shall but say: fulfillment implies no opposite.

But what about a world principle that would do away with "specific difference"? wouldn't one be right in seeing such clearing away as "spiritual democracy", that is, for the sake of imposing on a world order incapable of right moveents the notion of "numerical difference"?

If there's longing for confraternity with the angels, then every movement a man makes to establish such is a movement toward specific difference.

The differential world is the glorified body.
The world is prison—
I'm allowed to walk about—
No one knows me—
Or better they're told to shun me—
I gather flowers—
I reach out to birds—

From the standpoint of the world's own, there's no better way to "welfare" than the one that engenders a feeling of repugnance toward nature.

Following again the way downward, you come to an impasse that shows you to yourself as the maker of your own obstacles—but once clear of the impasse, which presupposes that the way out is thru the realization that accuses oneself, an image of deeper clarity comes thru: you as victim.

Why again the dread? is it true that the exclusion will take place shortly? You know that they can't harm you—if you order yourself properly, no circumstance that tends to bow can truly overcome—remember, the city has no intrinsic power, I mean, it can't act upon you unless you place yourself in a position of passivity—do you mean to say that the city's in the same position?—yes! its principle of movement seems to be general consent, that is, given an extreme populous honorabilis apparent virtual interiority must follow—but what about the general consent: how did it come about?—the answer is obvious: to turn away from God is to turn toward self—yes! and the city's founded on self-reliance; from this it's safe to say: the State, the Material Ideal, is the Self *magnified blown up a thousand times*—now that you know this you can walk anywhere and feel no oppression—but the impossibility of relations that brings a man to the realization that each man moves toward specific difference, turns the movement upon itself, leaving him groveling in darkness, gathering to himself a justification that is metaphorical: that is, the darkness that releases one from heat—but you know that this is impediment; therefore, release yourself from feelings of oppression.

No identification is possible when a man says: see the child standing by the window looking out at the rain.

What good is it to see the drunks sprawled out on the sidewalks, if your seeing can't go beyond, that is, to gather them up and feed them—does it do you any good to go away sorrowfully—the injustice writhes at the root; therefore, do your work of transformation.

To use *you* is to imply *I*—

Every time?—

Yes—

Then why the distinction?—
Call it a circle—
Persons in dance—
Motion is its first principle?—
It depends—
Go to a wood—
Find a pool—
Look into it—
There's no more wood—
There's heaven—
Totally light—
Do you mean it's buoyant?—
You see pun—*I* don't—
But to see heaven in a pool is not to see heaven—
The moment you looked into a pool to see heaven was the moment you in heaven saw a man looking into a pool to see heaven—

"I've seen you walk along the markets by the waterfront—you don't buy—I hardly ever see you walk the neat streets."—"You don't always see me—but it's true! I prefer the streets that look like time."—"That's a strange simile: aren't all streets involved in time?"—"Yes!"—"And wouldn't one be right to say: old street—anteriorly contemplative; new street—posteriorly active? And also respectively: back; front?"—"Yes!"—"Then give up the old streets—go over to the new streets."

"Time is always old—new time is 'here one momen gone the next'—future time is similar, that is, the only difference is: it's just a little ways up the river; therefore, time can't be anything but old, that is, circular."

"You were wrong from the start—no man can be serious in this society—yesterday, for instance, I heard an illiterate in front of an office building ranting about the injustice of the people in 'high places'—he said to be phoney is their motto and they want their workers to follow suit."—"The illiterates make sense—once I heard a drunk amidst fashionable street say: I'm right everybody's else's wrong!"

"Ornament is beside the point: is the world ornamental?"—"No!"—"Then how can you say that the world is prison?"—"I meant in so far as it is 'strapped in'."—"Then society is ornamental?"—"Yes! however, I prefer the word State."—"Do you mean that the State is society's stance?"

Remember that the Occident takes its force form the Fall.

To say "total light, therefore, total vision" is to say more than any proposition, because one *knows* wherein the *place* is angelic.

You hear: is the converse true of to use *you* implies *I*? and if so, does it alter the stuff that follows? to tell yourself that it is true and that the stuff that follows does remain constant is to hear: a yes or no tips the scale....

Beware of the moon mirrored—in water? what about the back black fender of a parked car?

A drifting out toward open sea—
Open window—
Angel—
Beloved—
Words gathering around a word—
Cliffs under moon—
Birds lighting—
Sun under tree—
Downtown the journey—
Upward the bird—
Blazing forth the journey's downward under tree—
Beyond open window sea—
Between open window and sea angel—
Beloved's the word that gathers the world to himself and then upward fulfills—
Awaken to see neither open window nor open sea—
See the stars from the burnt hill—
Awaken the city—
Sing the stars—

Cry out to the angels above the city—

Sing the stars the angels the angels the stars—

When you find yourself looking out of a window—the last night of the day metaphorically in the position of a shepherd leading sheep toward the darkness that is no more than a step—then every ache that is memorial comes before you, and, because of the possibility of a future intending breakdown, you sorrow as if renewal were but deceptive action, that is, a mask revealing a reality everywhere un-resolution.

"Why pay any attention to a future no where in your power—that is, if you know that time is old, therefore, circular, then you're already in a position that has nothing to do with it—therefore, walk in the light knowing that there is no impediment."—"But today I see only death."—"Then I can only say: you are blind!"

It is the intensity of activity that impedes contemplation; therefore, any system that pretends to release even tho enslaved is one that seeks to get the most out of you without incurring the loss of profit that comes from revolt.

Poverty seems to be the only action capable of reducing an intensity of activity.

"Are you seeking future things?"—"An intelligible metaphor for in the world but not of it is: if one finally contains place, then to be in it is tautologic."

on
  a
bridge

behind
  branches
an

angel—
  a
memory

of
  sea
a

longing
  for
home

scattered
  by
the

dance

no
grass
no
trees

a
block
of
homes

cars
speeding
by
in

rain

Behold the hill
And beyond
Against a wood
The birds above

The burning grass

lie
  down
angel
  broken

at
  the
wing—
  the

river
  flower
below
  you

withers
  by
the
  wood

so
close
the trees
birds

and
grass
along the
river

ending
below
this hill
my

home

                    there are

the children linked arm in arm on
the circle of green
                  and in the midst:
a tree

a beginning of snow
and in a garden
in moonlight
an angel

inwardly radiating

under
  the
branches
  above

the
  water
from
  the

hill
  beyond
the
  wood

a
  flower
in
  sleep

shaking

the

dust

off

the

feet

and

yet

smiling

the

angel

passed

thru

the

city

and

moved

up

and

down

trusting

in

the

path

    Night longer
than usual
vision plainly
lost
music
evidently
best
under streetlight
little else
to communicate
sound draws them in
the circle
the fire
the rose
back from walk
remembering the reading
nepenthe
coming in after 9
a long table simulates
committee room
room again
furnished room
sorrow futile
to move
city
seeks to
bow
or balance in a way
indifferent to either
extreme
sit amid the ashes
cry out
stars listen
woods give back

    Words
hills
woods anciently
sung
overheard
from under a wall
reveal
a depth
the voice
another man
given up to himself
pondering
reflecting
you

Reflecting
traffic
a window
of the corner house
shaded by the only tree
on the block
fails to reveal
the tugs
going toward
the opposite
shore

    Almost for three weeks
the same walk
theaters
markets
warehouses
coat old
lining torn
returning
facing the wind
the water to the right
memory

    Cast
into
darkness
words
meaning little
people wandering about
no flower
no hill

    Then over to waterfront
ships
and beyond
hills
and everywhere
falling
snow

Crystals

The new man is always the spiritual man.

We, too, conceive of contemplation as the activity that is wholly compatible with His City; therefore, the act poverty that moves us in that direction is in no sense negative. What we are trying to say is this: to live in God is to be contemplative.

It is wrong to think of contemplation as the opposite of activity: that is, contemplation is a prefiguration of the very activity that pertains to the Kingdom of Heaven. It is the State that fosters the idea that contemplation is passive, therefore, more in keeping with the man who doesn't work, or better who won't contribute to the give and take that is the market. From this it is just to ask: what is the meaning of the word activity when the State is Unity? it's obvious: exploitation.

How can we know life when to measure and to name pertain to determinations wholly our own!

Now what is this problem concerning knowledge: that is, is there any? We cannot place it in words; but even to say *that* is to place the statement in the intention rather than in the real: does this bring us before a background ever changing the moment we start to move toward it?

There is knowledge! and it's of the kind that makes a man see the whole world as the work; therefore, to love the work is to be face to face (would it make much difference if you were to say: to see face to face?).

It all amounts to this: if a man is capable of knowing completely, then his companions are the angels.

To say that a man's knowledge is face to face is to say that the vision is never at odds with the life.

A man need not formulate in such a world: that is, where the vision is never at odds with the life truth can never be an approach.

If truth can never be an approach, then what is it?

The beatific vision brings the world face to face with the Truth.

In the meantime, what do we do?

Aquinas says: "Et in rebus quidem corporalibus apparet quod res visa non potest esse in vidente per suam essentiam, sed solum per suam similitudinem; sicut similitudo lapidis est in oculo, per quam fit visio in actu, non autem ispsa substantia lapidis. Si autem esset una et eadem res, quae esset principium visivae virtutis, et quae esset res visa, oporteret videntem ab illa re et virtutem visivam habere, et formam per quam videret."

The hierarchical orders of the Church can only be valid metaphorically; therefore, every movement toward specific difference is the church's movement toward its proper prefiguration.

A man's proper prefiguration is his proper stance.

The ontological is still propositional. There isn't much that you can say about the real, except that it is: this makes one walk freely—that is, no system of thought or just plain system can overshadow him: therefore, if the argument is ontological, then any attempt to re-establish the natural is asymptotic.

Blake's argument against Analytics is an argument against himself: that is, the ontological is still propositional.

To be fair: to argue existentially or ontologically is to

argue incorrectly: however, the former at least stresses that knowledge is in the knower according to the mode of the knower, while the latter encloses existence in its insistence that it has grasped essence.

Blake's prophetic books still remain subservient to history —therefore, he places another generation in the position of a justifier of the ways of God to men: that is, another shall write of him in the way he wrote of Milton.

One has the feeling that Blake's final image of the new heaven and the new earth is an entangled image—that is, there's something discontinuous about it.

Now that you've said that Blake has spoken all the old truths, remembering what his argument against another was, release him and call him friend.

It came to me in sleep; Blake's Four Zoas is an attempt to square the circle; therefore, the indication is ad infinitum.

Blake never released himself from Homer—that is, his battlefield is the homeric plain.

From such a *plane* you can only get heroic type—that is, our "contention ... with dominion ... principalities" is still to be at the mercy of the gods.

The old truth is historical truth.

Since the Material Ideal is not out there with the force of

nature, then it follows that its mode of being comes from a reasoning that is ontological.

The resolution of the possibility of a spiritual art is: *isn't* is never valid except in relation to thought.

Riemannian space retains the notion of the horizontal in its confrontation with the unbounded.

A mathematical universe is equilibrated when its formulation is complete; therefore, any substantiation that is existentially presupposed is a consequent rather than an antecedent—that is, the latter is apparential.

This argument has nothing to do with existence or nonexistence—its concern is this: the possibility of a progressive formulation, that is, every possible temporal relation solved the universe is solved (it is obvious that the statement *the universe is solved* releases the word possible from any meaning).

Is there any meaning in a formula complete enough to represent a universe in the round?

To be drawn into the market only intensifies one's sense of the ambience that impedes; therefore, any science that pretends to have discovered a means to a re-establishment of the natural has, in truth, simply proposed to the mind an end that places the whole populace in a position conducive toward complete service to the State.

The despair: to say *the* world is to give rhetorical definitiveness to *your* world.

It is obvious that the notions *making it on your own* and *being responsible* are there solely for the sake of stressing the eternitiy in the now.

Lingusitics is the sole study of the logomachist.

Looking out only to refer back and then finally looking out significantly.

A doctrine is only valid ontologically, that is, nothing that one man or another can say can place the meaning unequivocally there rather than here. What is intended is a boundary that reduces each man's movement to a movement essential in the sense that the ambience is but a projection of his inner state.

Am I dead? My pulse
Still beats, and my eyes
Do not suspend:—
O my people,
My earth, my seraphim!
There's none to mourn me.

It is as it were sorrow
to walk these streets
where, after supper,
one, looking back, sees
the diner in the shadow
of a bridge—

Are there joys, friend,
  when light
    comes from no day?

Minds die this way;
  wilt from
    their own heat.

I hear of Ren's
illness—and hope
this concern

finds him
up an around
hungry for cookies

and tea; and ready
for romping
in snow—not yet?

then, at least,
at the window
watching

his playmates
belly-whopping
down the hills

below Mt. Hiei

l'envoi

Go, song, to Will and Ami;
tell them of my concern; be
graceful in your phrasing;
try to speak of melting snow.

here's
a
cherry
spray

for
each
of
you

—could
n't
find
any

birds;
they've
flown
to

woods

light
over
leaves
above
water
where
a
sight
of
sloping
green
breaks
thru

a
  river's
flow

a
  fall
of

leaves
  from
the

hills
  slop-
ing

toward
  its
banks

the wood's clearer
because of the children
gathering flowers
along its paths

Passing by the slops past the El
past the blossoming
apple-trees
a man
turns down a street
to factories
and then up
to homes
looking toward weeds
along tracks

   Quarter
moon
car
turning corner
rear view
window
five storey
trucking
co.

So Close

against light you my wife gather flowers along
the river reflecting hill and forsythia
  at night, your fragrance dissolves metaphor

in the midst of the collapse our room dark our
speech our love the background

our bodies naked given up to each other reveal
the ecstasy the earth

the world a river flowing reflecting light revealing
a river flower the world reveals our love in love

your odor returning night the bed our love returns
sea our first year

body to body our night less boundary than fragrance releases bird hill river

Quadrifariam

Contents

The Triune
227

Euphrasy
277

Via Negativia
307

Unitivia Via
321

Paradiso *Canto Primo*
331

Anamnesis
339

Marginalia
373

Anti-Hero
403

Intaglio
435

The Triune

I walked conversing with angels—
trees to the right
animals to the left
the path beyond quiet—
we moved toward the animals—
they moved with us toward flame
the quiet
then the air changed
the right reflected the left
and the movements ceased—
my spirit vanished beyond the hill—
birds flew up from the trees above the river
then night
wind
The creation
close
revealing no trap
man and woman
close
the leaves shading
their movement past water toward hill
Angels above water—
we came down the hill the sun beyond the trees—
we talked with men and woman
their light not from themselves
nevertheless radiant the branches glinting
from their nearness—
we continued along the paths
No journey draws significance from the encyclopediac
Destitute of references the seeing
gathers to itself always the proper
never once recalling impediment
in love therefore center or edge
meaningless
the sun setting behind us

Taking the path beyond the water
we came to a field
more people
some looked at us
others turned away
the background the sea
we passed lilies climbed the hill to the right
Circle whose center was no where visible except as
circumference presupposed itself as center to a
circumference no where visible
Then turning to the left the sun setting
we walked toward the wood beyond the river
people under a tree were speaking of women and
children wandering in deserts—
continuing along path
we met a man sitting against a rock
he was blind
he talked only of the ancient world
we knew the stories—
before entering the wood
I could still hear his song
Resolution the hill
the light
nevertheless out of deference
scattered flowers along the paths
then down to the right above water
came to a clearing—
already late morning—
we took the path to the desert
We sat in a garden
a reflection of star mountain leaf
the paths quiet
wind
music
body

No resolution possible
the sentimental gradational
therefore primitive
nor if differential
an opposite
I walked along buildings
up ahead a park and apartments beyond
left and right rivers
the geographical false
stressing a position
a totality as it appears in imagination
this not to say
a totality present
the vision differential
The park quiet
I climbed rocks
came to paths to bridges
to grass trees beyond
turned down to a lake
few rowboats out
some boys their pants rolled up
fishing at the edge
then up to a hill
the path to the street beyond the playground
I came to theaters
the crowds the shops
a complement
in memory
in the grove above the river angels
we passed animals
the odor the grass
we sat on a bank
the sun rising
then to warehouses
the waterfront a block down

We sat on a rock
people passing by a wood
the water reflecting a hill
memory the city
returning the man
the bench
old men drunks
the lovers under a tree
then we walked along the river
turned to the right
the path to a wood
animals tired
groping we came to a clearing
a man and a woman lying amidst grass
to the right mountains
the sun rising
Night
the river quiet
people sorrowing
their words revealing the old
the community
a man bowed near water
the wood above
we came to a hill
implication the reflection
then water reflecting hill
hill no longer implication
Up over rocks to a field
the sea below
then to the right
a ledge to the shore
stars
cliffs
memory
dust

Dying to the contemporary
the walk again
involving rain the vision
the exhaustion unable to resolve itself
the memory
people discussing
alienation
the ambience failing
to fulfill each person differentially
a woman's words
if you spoke to me more often
wind
a slope forsythia
the afternoons
walks for miles
a word one word
if you spoke to me
I wouldn't be so lonely
night
the car lots
better a movie a bar
the return
home the darkness
oak
the chimes
restoring the man
we stood in a park
looking up at
the big clock
my wife
my children
altering the words
the neons skyscrapers
warehouses
past

We came to flowers the river to the left
a grove up beyond the rocks
people down from a wood
then turning to the right
looking back
the last man and woman
past branches
the sun behind them
we went toward grass
the river a metaphor
Sitting in a garden
imagining the wood
a curve
the up and down
a circle
I wakened to a grove
the light seeking its own
the sound evoking entanglement
companionship the dream a longing
Then down the opposite side
no wood
no people
the path curving to desert
mountains
Again
the garden
melody
bird
the light
angel
shadow
the rhythm foreign
no profundity
history
then out past lilacs to sea

Leaf
wind
hill
the forms
shadows amidst water
the hill past
bird
water
then under branches
the light
the pool
then down to a river
the sun setting
mountains
the left the right
death
Odor
angel
my room
memory
willow
the branches above the path to orchard
the speed the universe
a trace
sleep the awakening
the man
the street
then the room
dawn
another awakening
space
the withering a reflection
the self
the beyond
quiet

Contemplating the wood sloping toward the lake
the confrontation
morning
evening
then toward desert
the horizon
the reduction the self
the man reflected the person
the wood
another
then the reflection
light
the identification logic
the outcome
flower
melody a consequence
light
diamond
fire
water
one
then branch
bird
river
implication
street
room
reiteration
the man passing a lot
the El a block up
word
the totality
fault
the gaze
impediment

In exile stressing sound
cars
the room
the environment
heredity
a joke
two people staring each other in the face
child furnished room
the mackinaw
the recurrences
carnations
sweet peas
the graveside
then water
space a reflection unity
light to river
the flowers planets
the universe a body
an obviation
horizon
I went toward a valley
water
light
a reflection rocks
the awakening a garden
dream
depth the illusion
river
lilacs
beyond the hill
animals in the grass below the paths to the mountains
a memory snow
a walk home
streetlights
the barges a guess

Light
under
branches
a pool reflecting hills
an angel moved toward a field
the metaphor flame
dying
the periphery a figure
space
sapphire
every surface revealing the petals withering
Passing beyond to water
mountains reflected
we turned to the wood to the left
people up amidst grass
old man by water
the children behind the hills echoes
the stars no
the moon no
the reflection no
eternal
Then impasse
star
sea
under willow past hill
background
mind
Bird
universe
edge wood
room
the literal
vision
dawn
branches indistinguishable

Seeing children in the midst of a valley
the stars wood beyond wood beyond a river
the seeing signifying
a loss angel
I continued up a path
the movement circular denying the universe
Back street
drunk
nickel for the child
a year before
iron bedstead
shadeless window
the corner candy store
the freight yard the slope a transformation
then to a garden
snow from the hills
the burden years
then out
down to a river
Ocean to the right
lilacs past
I walked under an El
the vision
window
street
backyard
tracks
shop windows
apartment houses
lots
crowds
oak
stoop
dynamo
trolleys 25 years ago

Trembling from the death I longed for
the background increasingly the self
occupations streets to sea
I dreamed wood
men and women shot among the trees
to the right of a waterfall
a girl raped left naked
grass stream
the man pausing
looking back
laughing
before going down the hill
the images cinematographic
journalistic
the national everywhere individual
the resolution a clearing
the crimes entanglements
the wood the city
then waking
I went out into the street
the city peaceful
prosperous
the newsstands
war
crime
diversion
the architecture positions
the people individually met belying the peace
the structure the inculcation
the warehouses
another time
the dock workers
the drunks
victims
nevertheless patriots

Flowers
angel
below the hill
dawn
my quiet
death
body
straight line
curve
one the other
other
reflecting
open going forward
lie
identity a person
dying
depersonalization
contradiction
fact reason
the sea
stars
universe
shadows
mind the light
false
the tree
snow
root
odor
bird similar
unity
vision
river
hill
dialectical

Then light a resolution the wood below a wake
the disentanglement
a woman gathering hill flowers
the spirit uninvolved
the words civil
the presuppositions
motion
creation
projections
the theme
creation no beginning no end
integrity
harmony
radiance
old
today equally old
the difference
the state
unity
we turned toward the hill
space
time
mind
then world
Darkness
music
trees river
the birds
animals
flames
the grass
crystals
the downward movement
comedic
the other resolution of the gradational

Death
the memory
shadow
then river
mountain
grove
past
wood recurrence
angel
leaf
light
revelation
star
hill
a man and a woman naked above the grass
the beyond transumptive
shadows of vine leaves
begrudged
gods references
the heavens fields
the man wakened
dream again implicative
foreknowledge the purpose
giant the universal body
total
then a pool
dawn
an angel down to a valley
odor
radiance
involvement
knowledge
a hill
forsythia
the gift

One and others juxtaposed
ambience conchoidal
the unitary unjustified
line spectral
point zero unresolved
unit not zero
however no negative no positive
positive stressed
subject attached to negative
Rain
I left the park
walked uptown
drunks
shops
side streets
trucks warehouses
vision
angel river
dusk
I continued turned right
galleries
order
generation
perfection
the generations
displacement
heretics
wanderers
our turn to be burned
our prosody
necessary
contingent
being presupposed
if not work
world as Idea in need of renunciation

The man dying the hill flame
the person reflected
people reflecting reflected
then going on
we went up to a wood
rested at the edge
star
field
sea
goat
lion
tiger
deer
insect
sand
cliff
eagle
river
flamingo
particle
desert
grove
sparrow
snow
oak
garden
gull
weed
moon
lake
valley
crystal
dust
words from the self
the pit justifying flame least providential

Angel under willow
fire below by river
road
valley
odor
reduction
the man a reflection
the god involution evolution
resolution deceptive
induction deduction
transformations
therefore equilibration
then opposite
generation
circular movement squared
the confusion
street
river
the failure
flower
foot
the withering
water
bird
branch
hill
grove
mountain
above
beyond
behind
background
the instinct
that
the habit foreground

Inward
the rose
revealing
light
resolving
melody
eagle
revealed
the person
reflecting
the man
on
a
hill
revealing
sea
then
heavens
vast
close
diamond
reflecting
the reduction
lily
then
fire
point
resolution
conic
elliptic
the balance
field
the
flowers
rays

Glass light then hill rocks past beyond up

Light
star
garden
dream
melody
body
upper
lower
differential
desire
consideration
planets
numbers
approximations
least
limits
first
no
memory
image
absorbed
vision
reflective
no
figure
figurative
letter
merit
least
charity
first
body
glorified
work
intelligential

Thru wood beyond hill
people
valley below
dusk
reflection
leaf
water
cliffs past
eagle
angel
grove
vision
rocks
grass
river
then down
path
the awakening
pool
dawn
dream
sea
space
universe
maximum
minimum
completion
exclusion
contingencies
therefore
collapse
system
the self
closed
exclusive

Spirit dream when least is flame
gathered to itself child
walked hills
knew memory
collapse
looked far
sought beloved
strength
knew also wood
cry
day everywhere
dark
light
mind
therefore equally
dark
continued
valleys
no rest
child lost
rose
lily
up
down
bowed
came to river
vanished
beyond
angels
animals
heavens
quieter
child
gathered
up

Path
below
hill
river
below
path
wood foreground
then no hill
path
river
wood
rather bird branch above sea
then puddle
drinking fountain
foreground path
background hill
people right
trees left
then the dying
not the flame
wind not wind
the outcome
no self
spirit
ambience
the man amidst field
his companions
angel
animal
equally amidst
his wife reflecting rays
eternity
themselves nothing
the spirit
everything

However individual
nevertheless separate
absorbed
field other
angel flame
space
absorption collapse
other dreaming angel
angel metaphorical
flame anagogical
space literal
literal absorbing field
other consideration
either from standpoint
of infinite in extension
or finite in size
or from the totality
constituting unification
world postulate
reaps no a priori privileged position
therefore
solution
integration of the imaginary
depending upon transformation
of n-dimensional
differential
formal
of finite
infinite whose eternity
resolution of linearity
curvilinearity
therefore only possible
science
every sense
foundational

Lilacs
moonlight
melody
far off
people willow
the man less reflective
pool dream
noon
child
lot
each side homes
melody
close
then square
consideration
space
spirit
flame
lily
transformation
equilibrations
false
melody
closer
sapphire
universe
not body
body universal
melody
closest
vision
immediate
not correspondent
path
exaltation

Abstracted from sense
sense river
an awakening
not completely
released
from the image
river-bank
attached itself
to another ground
consequently
image
always there
simply consequence
because extension
ground
discovered
never ground
originally
forsaken
therefore image
river
gathered to itself
moon
woods both sides
a man
his image
child
eternity
reflection
ground
identical
sense
then illumination
senses
unimpeded

Wood
then
up
path
hill right
sea beyond
then
down
rocks
path left
grove
below
hill
valley
between
hill
mountain
valley
then
desert
between
mountain
hill
sea
hill
sea
mountain
resolution
therefore
valley
desert
sea
reduction
wood
self

Eternity
visually never
glint
branch water
nevertheless
glint
branch water
eternal
Rocks along brook
animals left amidst grass
people above in wood
angel turned right
gathered light
reflected
people
animals
rocks
along
left amidst
above in
absorbed
wood
grass
brook
opposites
transformed
others
absorbed
therefore
angel completely
light
cause
brook
grass
wood

Leaf revealing water
reflected
angel
reflecting
water
revealing
hills
woods
lake beyond
dark
everywhere light
everywhere
closed
reflecting
fall
revealing
linear
bird
shadow
ocean
shore extension
intension
collapse
city
visually
crystalline
revealing
reflecting
angels
animals
revealing
a man
his reflection
person
trapped

Spheres ground
air not air spirit
angel moved freely
each planet
different
however
size orbit
apparent
heliocentric
given up to
theocentric
more
less
altering
revealing
differentially relating
equally participating
Reflection
refraction
wake
pool
foot
mountain
wind
one image
tree
river below
wood above
tree reflected
tree reflecting
therefore
light
tree
considering itself
image shade

Eternity image
procession
coterminous
procession grass river
hill background
anagogical
continuity number
significance procession
Sat amidst green
branches right
against hill
river left
valley beyond
valley hill
beyond hill
hill then branch
against light
mountain beyond
close
flame one
identification procession
other two identification
anagogical
light
beyond hill
branch against
sun
number defined
then went up hill
vanished
flame
hill
branch
coterminous
allegorical

Drifted
only islands
farthest stars
sought
haven
cliffs
seabirds
nothing
horizon
everywhere
hovering
Language ambience
word allegorgical
sense anagogical
sea object
hill
gift
use
Valley
angel
flame
river
beyond
wood
wood bird
above
hill
greater bird
boundary
beyond
spheres
tragic then
gaze
flower turned toward fire
eagle

Wind
wood
stood
edge
odor
panther
leaf
glint
sun
branch
walked
water
fire
fire
hill
water
hill
beyond
lilies
stars
movement up
down other
taciturn
passed
angel
labored
physiognomic
wall
spirit
earth
animal
flower
bird
inner
dead

Light other light angelic
light toward light
completion
delineation released
termination existent
flow non-existent
existence non-existence combined
combination bounded
finitistic
Found a bench
sat
watched traffic
the fall an awakening
or given an ascent
a sleep
making
doing
interdependent
cause
architecture
self to self mind
efflorescence
vision full
everything else empty
vague
necessary
poverty the gift
the city man
dreamer
poet
an image
center
no guide
invocation
useless

Seeking to recover the fragrance the hill
we took the path left of a grove
the people below behind the trees
sitting facing the river
our words
dust
in conflict over thought image
the discursive a point in favor of criticism
if intellect imagination were not one
one other to another
other one to itself
persons gathered up
re-defined
the lake defining the man
the suicide
water flow above me
cover me eternally
tense pointless where ground resolution of everywhere
the point rather desire
our wood
our city
light interwoven
river sea
we may never return
the epical falsification
impermanence
humanity split
work leisure
an arrangement
suiting the profiteers
in the wood then dark
light flower word successive transformations
effaced
song vision body face to face
radiating in radiance

Trees around water the man climbing hill
diminution increment memorial
movement if any then all
differential horizon
image stone illuminative
stone fact divided
vision to vision progressive not progressive
paused
looked back
desert
melody determinant
desert then bird
hillside dead leaf dust gathered
Beyond hill bird flower
rejuvenation
rays
river
children unobstructed
perceptual intelligential
educative tautologous
connatural complemented
hill
beyond
behind
aspectual
hill no aspect spiritual
the man ascending vanishing
trees
water
altered
reflected
reflector
one not one
hill behind dominant

Spirit the spirit an identification
water an image significantly subject
the revelation the man
resolution the projection
the man another an extension the one below
If point no boundary
then point invalid
metaphorical
the man reference
the universe creation
eternity
image
use
relational
fire
plain
angel
visional
plane other
close
far
approximations
speed apperceptive
rest background
the relation
circular
each to each
however
differential
integral
appetitive
the noetic
self
return
pilgrimage image eternity

Grade not grade the formal the inclusive
ontology the third
the second intelligence
the first memory
spirit recalling understanding itself
the man inward
light
pool
soul to mind
eternity
therefore memory anteriority
the sentimental wood
the spiritual principle
the civil myth
impediment
generation corruption
snow
wood
moon
adumbrations
language
self
things
polemical
always city
the poet
citizen
forgoing the word
audience wake
redirected
orientation spirit
identification the third
the second
the first
released the soul informed contemplative

People
then snow
the climb less concatenation
than realization
fall
the antithesis justifiable
if illumination
the difference
totality inductive forgone
below beyond river angel
background wood
self
darkness
both
either
neither
both
neither
resolving
either
therefore
both
neither
either
released
no where argument
the angel beyond
below
below fall
friend
wisdom spirit
the spirit both
division boundary
not light
but song if song principle

Thru mirror in enigma
sea
vision word identity
inner sound darkness
inner vision light
darkness prefiguring light
deafness unsealed
word snow
gravidity
past work returning
not unresolved
rather same word appearance
contingencies
the relation
word finally one
not itself
the dying balanced
the spirit realization
the work the word
unity
full
then the flickering
edge
sea
height
depth
effaced
plain burden
sea universe
crystal
the ethical
meaningless
work word revitalized
signification
vision neither in nor out

Sea no horizon teleology
background
intensification
past
the heroic
the proletarian
an identification
if the intelligential
the movement
the relation
therefore the thelogical
use the gift
the clarification
background
intensification
species
image
then rock
a boy below amidst grass
the father on a bench
the hills beyond intelligences
spheres undivided
the hierarchical
apparential
the eternal
integral
river
plain
hill
valley
processional
father
son
eternity
image

Light
intelligence
light
hill
pool
concave
convex
mind
crystal
return
presupposition
center
angels
water
objects
transcendentals
forms
undefined
experience
individual
universal
identity
eternal form
supposition
image
shadow
trace
informative
lover
contemplative
speculation
participative
reason
visional
beatific

Turned left
wind
willow
passed river beyond lilacs behind hills
reached plain
horizon abstractive
past
infinite
Beyond
forsythia
angel
hill
left
path
right
then
path
left
hill
right
beyond
angel
forsythia
finally
circle
the
indentity
form
life
invalid
work
a
means
therefore
definitive

Euphrasy

the street the reflection

the window

the waking

to backyard

snow

moon

sunrise—

the silence greater because of the roofs

this way that way
relieved by either
either way
or neither way

returns to itself
as boundary
positive in its way
unbounded

    To a man
waiting to cross a street
a reflection
of water reflecting
hills stars moon
stars hills
woods
reduces itself to a reflection
completely crystalline

autumn wind
unfathomable sky
river
cup

Morning and Evening Portfolio

two movements

lyric

dramatic

the opening

sorrow

the 2nd

coaxes the spirit

toward temple grounds

not forgetting a stage

illusory enough

to present city

the 3rd

brings close the cry

then moves

the spirit to guess at

the twofold aspect

of the river-god

enter angel

the 4th

so delicate

the spirit brightens

a clearing

reality

no stage

then stage

already resolution

the 5th

the orient the glint

beauty

recasting even the emptiness

the block

the dandelion

not yet in flower

the 6th

waterfall

mountain

drapery

the dying

close

the print

vast

the world

balanced nevertheless

the lower arc

implies indefinable

curve

then hill

continuing implication

of the dying

the 7th

the hovering

the stage

trembling

revealing the sea

in tension

not itself

maybe bird

seeking to wreck itself

yet

the children

quieting

always there

in integrity

the 8th

the drapery

fluttering

and then rock

preparing

the spirit

the 9th

resolution of the dying

the birth

the up and down

and then finally

the pyramidal

the shape

reevaluating the stage

"the page relation"

    lying close to lilacs
the sun going down
behind the hills
an angel walking in the valley
a man wakes
and from the tree by the river
to the left
birds flying down
to a grove

last leaf fallen
an angel turns to the sea
drifting
withering

center dark
circumference light
and beyond
equally
dark
light

again the bird flies up—

melody

the land

Via Negativa

Rain
bitterness
I can know nothing but dissatisfaction
this means my knowledge
is negative
it sees no gift worthy of respect
it looks to no writer
because no writer of this age
for instance is worthy
of respect I mean
whether of the underground
or the upper world
the writer the artist what have you
invariably
spews sentiment
he knows no other action
he seeks even when it seems
he is for neither side
to promulgate a journalism
that must by every turn
demoralize
trap
a man
My hell
I emphasize my hell
where there is no other meaning but darkness
the rhetoric societal
leaving a man neither in nor out
that is either in or out
depending upon

another position
but since position is not part
of the meaning
in and out lack meaning
bearing to each other
significance
only if one is in
another out
But there is
love
yesterday
for instance
I walked the city
and yet not city
because outside of the city
my vision
walked
mystical
not mystical
more intelligential
good to walk in the city
and yet know
you are not in it
nor can ever be
therefore
you wonder
wherein is hate
I sit in a room
everything others get
I do not
but if to sit in a room
means my position
is precisely that
then there is no complaint
I listen to birds

then get up
and go out
to find birds
I seek parks
birds in trees
even tho trees
fewest trees of streets
interest me of course
as much as birds
in parks
2:30 in the morning
woke up
fright
took a shower
loneliness
a spiritual necessity
my room
done up
as if holiness
were ambience
Raised my head
no end to this writing
sentences
taking their significance
from infinite combinations
but when the writing has reached
its final word
the word reduces itself
to closed word
the closed word raised to another height
only if another extension is seen
which extension in turn
imparts
to everything that went before
the vision

no end
therefore book on book
death
horizontal
cardinal
vertical
ordinal
the wheel turned
death again
but you have this clarity
no one else
can solve the insoluble
Lilac odor
I looked up
vines literally draped over balconies
the image old
plain enough
the city cannot keep up with itself
the mania for renovation
equals
the mania for quaintness
but one's argument
is not with city
at least
not now
one knows better
I see my work as the solution
of the anti-hero
I am lower
poorer
more truly proletarian
the song
in but not of
released
by not even in

more given up to God than self
self least
because self only worthy
as branch is
to light

Love darkness
spirit
this
that
neither
but if love seeks
light
light
dark
dark
light
then know
negative
not negative
same
everywhere
but different if same
self
no where equal
more darkness
darkness separate
body
soul
no where one
each either
neither
other
one
neither
if one
other

If art is an intellectual habit, which is to say that the ambience is spiritual, then the notion of the concrete being fully determinable and literal is untenable.

The metrical unit is the fall.

Wisdom is the environs to which each man relates because each man reflects the other differentially relating, equally participating.

To refer to one's set of desirable objects is to refer to the senses—not the psyche. (One must remember that the movement of the senses is toward their proper objects of love.)

Personalism does not belong to a spiritual art.

The person is the man considered from the standpoint of the senses. This is only valid if: b is a + c (b = a + c): e.g.:
> if a is b (a = b)
> but b is a + c (b = a + c)
> then a is c (a = c)
>> a is not c (a > c, a < c)
> therefore a is not b (a < b).

To stress ethos is to stress separation.

Enlightenment has meaning only in Babylon.

Our position is intelligential—not mystical. But the not mystical is an instance of re-definition—not an obviation of the truth.

If one obsorbs the other, then the one loses meaning, because the identification is a relation reflective of the obviation: the other absorbed.

There is a point at which the first reduction of the Dantesque fourfold interpretation reduces itself to correspondence and identification, identification transforming correspondence in the sense that the letter is not a figure, the figurative referable to the letter.

Art (differential) Science (integral) complete the resolution. (Cf. *Crystals*—"The resolution of the possibility of a spiritual art is....")

The solution of Cantor's system of transfinite numbers, where $\omega\text{-}\upsilon=\omega$ says that υ is as distant from ω as $\sqrt{2}$ is, where approximation is never solution, is contained in our "the environs to which each man relates because each man reflects the other differentially relating, equally participating"—that is, given the solution $\omega\text{-}\upsilon=\omega$, it can only habituate us to a theory of transformations: therefore, correspondence revealing the extension, identification, we stress the ordinal, $\beta + 1 > \beta$ resolved in *veritas principaliter est in intellectu...*, that is, the greatest ordinal reduces to correspondence which at its deepest is the Self.

Cardinality and ordinality are aspects of a fundamental state relational in the sense that no other substance with respect to God is tenable.

(The fundamental state is the glorified body.)

To paraphrase Cantor: approximations tend toward the least, which is to say that the limits $\sqrt{2}$ and ω are the least of another order, that is, the first if we remember that $\sqrt{2}$ and ω are existences irrespective of approximations.

In the light of '$(p \lor q) \supset ((p \supset p) \supset p)$', Gödel's proof should have been more total—that is, given the disorientation of today's Science, the whole of Science is dominated by the non-derivative '$(p \lor q)$': therefore, every formally undecidable formula (proposition) is but a reflection of the more inclusive system completely non-derivable: that is, to prove the one non-demonstrable is to prove the other non-derivative.

It is now clear that a system non-derivable generates another ad infinitum by implication satisfying axiomatics.

If a man confronts the Gift the Holy Spirit, then this constitutes to some extent his identification with it.

Logic is not referable to application.

Illumination: *veritas principaliter est in intellectu, secundario vero in rebus* because of *secundario in rebus*.

Unitiva Via

mens intuetur per rationem, cum cogitat universalem essentiam
no poetics valid whose substantiation the space-time continuum

theological poetry Eternal Form because the indentification Use the Gift clarifies the background (the intensification) species in the Image

the glorified body the individual the universe
the indentification the individual the universal formal
individual universal an identification undefined
Spirit the spirit an identification

Paradiso *Canto Primo*

The Commedia is Eternal Form—not medieval art; therefore, any critical evaluation is out of question, because criticism is an orientation whose standard is not release but return, that is, pilgrimage is return but return in no sense an aspect of reduction, which is to say, any man approaching the Commedia should approach it humbly, seeking to attain that purity necessary to a movement whose resolution is everything that went before, that is, the Convivio is not denial ma maggiormente giovare per questa quella.

Maraviglia sarebbe in te, se, privo
   d'impedimento, giù ti fossi assiso,
   com'a terra qüiete in foco vivo.

   Invocation following upon the theme in una parte più e meno altrove—the memory unable to go beyond, that is, the vision fully satisfied, the language, means toward an end, inevitably turning back upon itself. Appollo invoked, the Poet reveals the Virgilian all'ultimo lavoro, the implcation being Beatrice as guide, resolving epical desire, the canzone justified, terza rima prosodic metaphor Dal centro al cerchio, e sì dal cerchio al centro: therefore, the foundation paradisaical, the projection is future, other poets moving similarly, relating, complementing.—Beatrice turns to the left, looks toward the sun: the gaze more fixed than eagle's—the Poet, pilgrim desiring return, reflects the gaze, gathering from it a transformation oltre nostr'uso. Tu non se' in terra…; the theme più e meno brought closer, that is, natural, sensitive, volitional, revealing the contemplative, the active in 'l ciel sempre qüieto nel qual si volge quel c'ha maggior fretta; the literal an aspect of the spiritual, the spirit no aspect, the Holy Spirit the spirit an identification. Since the creation inclines toward God, and given matter disposta e apparecchiata, the revelation is the metaphor: the creation form and matter perfectly in agreement, that is, from the standpoint of the artist, the universe is not impediment.

Anamnesis

moon   skyscrapers
moon   branches

blocked

blue everywhere
light ever
center
unseen
where yes
clearly
flower
not unlike
no

gardens
streets
not wretched
rather
state
projected
discoloring

sit in a park
otherworldly

the position Art is Life
reveals the contradiction
work as end in itself

I'm not struggling
whatever the movement
that's the way
God wants me to go

literature can only approach integration

the way is tragic
the resolution comedic

there can be no poetry
if the resolution is utopian

they want you to submit
to the other deceptive aspect
of the Material Ideal
comparative literature

therefore
to withdraw
from the literary world
is a must
this proves
our style no style
ars imitatur naturam
in sua operatione

it takes courage to go this way
because it is not the way of the world
I mean
the heretics
can no longer be
Luther
Bruno
Campanella
heresy is going against
the Material Ideal
and only the spiritual man can do that
but here going against
is innocuous
no trap
no argument
release
the Material Ideal not something to be destroyed
because the spiritual man not impeded
his movement reaps
enough daily to see thru
release even the Material Ideal

can there be a poetry of place
no
people
no
no poetry that seeks to release
even the Material Ideal
can be dramatic
epical
or
lyrical
then what kind of poetry is left
given the Hegelian
the Marxist
there can be no poetry
because the upshot is
the Platonic user
maker
no imitator
therefore
the kind of poetry
we postulate
is the kind that resolves
book
canzone
song
what kind is that
theological poetry

do I have a life
any recourse
to the natural
would seem to say
no

on my way back
from my parttime job
I think
have I written malice
because I have failed
to give lip service
to the civil
there are the workers
breaking their backs
the traffic
complements them
I'm the same
only I refuse to submit
my revolt
is not to give in
to any desire
that ultimately leads
to a justification
position achieved
society more fully reformed

then there's the home
I return to my wife and children
their existences
tied up
in the scheme of things
surrounding
how do I alleviate the burdens
I don't
I can't
I'm just a worker
and what is even worse
a poet
who sees his poetry
as work
a means toward an end
do I desire
to be anything other
than a worker
no
thus the tragedy
of my movement
any worker's movement
but the dialectical
is not the thought process
I'm involved in
if involvement
therefore
process
can in no sense
take significance
from a logic
not referable
to application

what about the political situation
it's misleading
of course
it depends upon
your position
in society
how else can you represent
your particular view
no report
can ever claim
to be ubiquitous
therefore
the uselessness
of the reports
they simply reflect
the position's slant
and of course
the Material Ideal
is the better for it
because the solution of
all these slants lies
in the integral
that knows no differences

how far can we go
in our descent
toward particulars
not far
our language
mathematical
or otherwise
just reaps surfaces

it is said that Art is useless
and that if useful
it must be social
and that if not social
then the User Society
cannot be in the position
that dictates

word it again
the imitator is in relation to
Use in the Gift
If this is so
then the notion of audience
takes its significance from
Spirit the spirit an identification
the final identification forgone
therefore
the theological poet
indirectly reveals
the user and maker
in harmonious relation to
the Holy Spirit
because the true object
of the theological poet
is Eternal Form
Species in the Image
the experiential

the senses of the audience
unimpeded
each member released
free to journey his own way
it must be so

the spiritual life is the real
nominalism can take no hold there either
therefore
since the poet's object
is Eternal Form
it follows
that the quieting
of epical desire
is an indication
of the transformation
of the tragic ache
for anterior time
fulfillment real
the tragic way
re-directed
in view of it
it goes without saying
that the comedic resolution
is not total
that's what constitutes
the realism
of the spiritual life

interesting how these same phrases
keep cropping up in my work
over the years
they're the same words
but the significance is different
is this the range of particularization
maybe so
but one thing is sure
God is the reason
and end
of all our movements
we bear witness to the Gift
the fact that work
is not an end in itself
gives us the insight
that our release from it
is not proof
of its uselessness
on the contrary
our release clarifies it
to an extent
that is truly definitive
does this imply
that the self
releases itself from work
only in the end
to look down upon it
that could be read into the release
but it makes no sense
if the release
is Eternal Life
the work Eternal Form
we live in and thru God
therefore
Eternal Form and Eternal Life
are not an identity
Eternal Form
taking its realization from
Spirit the spirit an identification
Use in the Gift

if the spiritual life is fulfillment
then the natural is participative
therefore
a spiritual art is full
altho the fullness
is not due to
the space-time continuum
from this it becomes clear
that the civil
can become like the natural
altho again
not in the sense of
the space-time continuum
because such a perfection
is ontological
an end in itself
which prevents the civil
from releasing itself
from *superbia*
it is true
however
that the civil fulfilled
is no longer the civil
but such a transformation
shows the reality no impediment
therefore
it is clear
how the spiritual artist
can use the natural

the underground is a mania for the particular

should I talk of branches
animals
where in my daily movements
am I met by the natural
no where is not the answer
but it does say
the exertion to stay
amidst the spiritual
is least
if a man knows
that the state is least
but that isn't true either
because if the state is least
then the knowledge of it
is not the cause
of the exertion
being least

a failure
my clothes prove it
my apartment will soon be demolished
yes
renovation

the other circle
circle
no
fulfillment
which
therefore
does away with the word other
draws up the circle
involved in impediment
transforms it
returns it to itself
a circle
no longer in contradiction

Marginalia

behind window
sea
beyond poplars
hill

gulls inland
wood right
sun setting

we live no enchanted life
only sea
yesterday
rose
leaves

dragon
sun ray
hold on
kids
wherever gold
blue

the fall of a great house
the body

horses
led
down
hill

stars risen

lying down
resting
not listening
nevertheless
music

no reason to be poetic
but I think
a lot about
our trip to the sea
the place we rented
for $20 a wk
no shower
the bed
pretty bad
room enough for only one

save the political theory
and throw out the rest

or

his work's a cover up
for his lack of experience

ocean
tomb
hearing bird
remembering
standing among trees
no where true
the hills neither behind either
forced back
death the preoccupation
lilacs sensed
cemetery
a boys obsession
the background

the extension of the walls
the senses
the converse
insensible
water
beyond trees
other times
between hill
grove
transformation
preventing
return

we stood on a bridge
the vantage point
a willow
eery

some nights
all we talk about

living outside the city
in a house
above a stream

so I don't know the practical world
I write
for angels

my sense of giving

intelligibles

I can give you no hand
if you wish to kill yourself
go ahead

lie toward the dark
the shade drawn

I'm a white horse
who's
going
to
die

a moment
the world
closed

image
signifies
release

thought
verifies
drawing
up
image

thought never far from image
image drawn up
release

sitting at a back table
in an automat
my glasses off

the window up ahead
setting sun opposite

the jobs
alienate
alienum

Anti-Hero

where
God
since no one accepts the work
—rest
unaccepted

if one denies most of the tenets of modern literature, then he's in no position to teach.

It is true that my withdrawal from the literary world is complete, but withdrawal can only mean desire of fame (vanity)—writing is not pride: to write for Humanity *God the Subject* alters every sense of the writer as *personality*: therefore, it is not the writer's job to seek out the latest innovations of the day—the principles of the craft are perennial; he has ancient teachers, and with them he silently converses.

If they consider you cold remote, the perennial rights you: near warm.

Not every man should love your speech, nor is it just that such a unanimity exist, but there is God Who insights the vision—more than enough for any man.

A wandering seeking new speech entia non sunt multiplicanda praeter neccessitatem.

The rage is gone, but the ambience remains the same.

Maybe this is the way it should be: the life empty for all purposes except the poetry that says God the vision everything lived thru not so bad after all: but this is true at the moment of writing; it has no meaning at the moment of living. Such a conflict can't be real; it must be imposed— from where? the outside. Does this exonerate the sufferer?

Words that suggest the country, leisure *despair*—why? because nothing in the life says that I can make it away from the market—my personality has become increasingly withdrawn—can't go anywhere without getting sick—the parties false to my way of thinking, and, of course, that isn't fair—people are entitled to fun, and the gloomy fellow is cancer—he's worth more if he at least knows *to check the feast* is not just.

Here you're just viewing yourself from an occasion belonging to the past—as you say: you're more withdrawn now than ever; and this is a sickness; however, the sense that seems to irk you most is that you still have a long way to go—if you were 60, you could breathe easier: at last it's over! but not yet 40, the spirit balks, doesn't have the strength to renew if withdrawal is acute.

The quiet I can't achieve comes to me at work only as a phrase. I may pause, look up from my desk toward windows fronting similar buildings, knowing that the freedom that supposedly belongs to the pedestrians has me as an onlooker, the secure position more secure behind bars.

The country and the city are wedded and no issue comes of it.

We don't take sides; we know that place is not the answer: if the education's sentimental, it affects all: and all the effects (sciences, arts) of the society do its bidding. Here's the desert of the modern saint!

After working in the prison yard, a man in his cell turns to his thoughts to hear deeply: God be praised!

The man moves, the angel illuminates, full common society the ground the Holy Spirit the foundation the Way toward final release.

Poetry draws none of its force from either in the city or in the country. Imagery in toto is species in the Image.

What is better than what a thing is like—even tho what is can only be gotten at suggestively.

If you're writing this for neither Church nor State, then what's the point? that somehow if a man can't do something worthwhile outside of these two folds, then the movements the relations are meaningless. Again: true work can only have for its vision the Eternal the *final identification forgone* the abstractive *useless*, that is, where the abstractive subsists the object never fully clear of the psychological.

Thus: the projections the set-ups impediments that reduce each work in one way or another to either of the above two collective representations of the Man; therefore, whether either dominates to the total eradication of the other or both join to form One the Man or exist side by side or together one a little more prominent than the other, it matters little to the spiritual man, whose *experience* is Eternal Life.

I am a slave seeking a corner at night to write.

A man thinks about universals while on the job, and the sense that comes thru most is no future worth it if the present diminutive.

What they can't take away from you: you've succeeded in establishing the postulate that original poetry is not far from original thought.

The mind gathers clutter not only from certain objects around it but from jobs seeking ever to burden. Returning home then is recovery. Who knows you on the job?

Exile or prison? both and music no where invoked bcause everywhere detrimental to deepest longing the crown resolving in exile in prison.

Should a writer gossip about his personal life?
autobiography
modern
false

If prosody is ideal, then the cause (motive) is the communal unrealized; if real, Spirit informs.

Intaglio

path to sunrise
tree midpoint

kids
bounding
down
from
rocks
hit
the
shore
forcefully
and
then
run
the
length
of
it

walking thru woods
coming upon lilies
the past life
a lake
        haunting

from above
under a tree
people huddled close
gloating over
a man losing his footing
grasping a ledge
unable to hold on
letting go

people
objects
the public square
infinite
space

sitting against a tree
amidst grass
the hill beyond
the sun's

the moon

a grave
by the path
past two pines
the archway

						I go up a hill and sit with my
children on a rock
								the tree below quiet more
center

passing to garden
then out among trees
the flowers gathered
              withering

sitting
        finding myself isolated in darkness
the room one single lamp before me
matching depth

I lived daily the spiritual
my meals taken alone
the reality false
the position
never ubiquitous
went to a coffee shop
the discussions
war
city
one said
war national
the other
city familial
both
therefore
nation
home
complement
other talk
folk singers approximate realities better
we are at the beginnings again
then the position of onlooker
uninvolved
not choice but birth
the language becoming less visional
yet at a certain level
whatever the word
the total vision reflective
then going on
reason
a loss
the spirit cut off
Spirit seeking the spirit
in grass love
light going

Remembering not discovering
if eternal
then body
glorified
mind
giving out
necessary
where body
given up
the suffering
an argument
the man descending
forgetting fall
investigation path
progressing
ascending
infinite straight line
returning
past eulogistic
end
future
dome
control
eradicating
present
mind
soul
body
entangled
in water
the pain
requiring light
blanching the eyes
informed
informing home

Turning
away
from
water
looking
toward
moon
evil
inhering
trees
homes
everything
beyond
then
near
dawn
a
conversation
a
minute
two
$20
too
much
the
prostitute
unconcerned
the
doorway
a
frame
the
hotel
lobby
empty

The future then and a death
arrived late
somewhere
near midnight
took the only rooms available
the horizon
sea
light as far as the door
the
shade
less
than
half
way
drawn
startled
went to the window
a
group
of
people
up
from
the
beach
outside
the
bar
across
the
street
turned away
the painting above the bed
a storm
ship going under

In a garden fronting sea
a man lingers
then moves toward a gate
the lingering a past
a recollection
admitting
no deeper experience
his certainty
deriving its sense
from the fall
and the working out
that is recovery

at the foot
of a mountain
a lion
groveling
wallowing

underground
no light
either end

in a dream
fell thru a hole
in a bridge
to my death

week day mornings
sealed in a room

buildings closing in
seemingly toppling

nearly dead
nevertheless
unperturbed

mountains hills
even
spheres boundaries
domain
freely given

a park poet ok a bum

    intuiting farthest light
standing in a grove
on a hillside
a man conveyed rays
to an angel below
facing sea
reflecting only
gull

lion
flame
beyond panther
then past oak
to plain

the shattering of glass
and the spirit worth less
than a speck of dust

    beat out the life
                        the earth
  giving way
                    to the sky

off 6th
        a graveyard

the willow presiding

ocean liner
gone behind
cliffs

the wake
however
still

glimmering

lying in a room facing a garden
a man turns inward to quiet
the quiet of the room different
more a counterpart
of the all day rain

leaving the window open
the living room all but dark
except for the patched light
on the fire escape

                    one path curving above
another
            the vision coming
                        into view
totally

sidewalk café
the avenue
           not
              a river

in passing

old doors
at the edge
of a lot

dying then
in the wave's
intenser
day

in contrast to the bright
day a junk shop and an
old lady in a rocker

looking down
at water
the thought
opposites
points joined
but to what
purpose
if the thinker
remains
poised above
water

I walk
looking up
at the full moon
the influence
working
unawares

easing the eye
scanning
 the offing

the train ready to pull out of the station
the fluorescent lights
for a moment
shooting stars

since the world is the State
and the State the Self
to escape the self
is to escape the Self
the world bearing the color
of the State

to vanish is to release
        the world

spiritually sapped
so bowed
by spring

getting off the sidewalk
into a doorway
the street
          a river
                    overflowing

sun or shade our talk
                         by river

lying about naked

morning intercourse

                              the aura

    highway along river

        rows of benches

                even closer

after eating our lunch
walked the boardwalk
broken
beer bottles
on the sand
perverse sideshows
for the kiddies
everywhere
under
        bluest
                sky

that headland's
a whale

even at night the city streets
    circles at cross purposes
  churn

alone on a road
the final trace

vain the grave
and no posterity
and an audience
a century off

sit before grass
know background
tho the seeing
acknowledges
no beyond

shadows of weeds on a rock
evening returning

object
    to
        object

Lumen Gloriae

Contents

Infinitesimals
507

Disigilla
581

Infinitesimals

settling

of the nature

of falling

unable to go on
illness and an afternoon
equally
      inevitably
            severing

I sit in a house
literally
falling about
my ears

the courts
weigh
the issues

deem
pros and cons
necessary

in poverty
    knowing nobody
water flowing in
    from all sides

riding a train

looking at homes

desiring a home

poor drunk
asleep on the sidewalk
clutching his penis

river
      warehouses alongside
a superimposition
eye noticing less in front
than behind

in one room
and for a second
in another

just a doze

transfixed

seeing flow
in the light
on the floor

ashes

even so

odor

essence

space

my state
            down
                to
                    a
                        t

                            .

bird
      gliding
beyond
hill

below

wanderer

existing no place
pilgrim no staff
entering no space

in light spirit to spirit
recalling deeper light
communicating deepest
sight

universe closing behind
pilgrim beyond
even
one with point

    an old man leaning out of a window
knowing himself useless
        the potted plant beside him
backing it up

candlelight
and the shadow
of the base
of the candle
holder
      at rest
             circling

going down to the river
I look across to the hills
my spirit in union
triumph over opposites

roof seeming horizon
approach verifying
metaphor

for Dolores

as I work
hang upon my neck
or look in
leaning upon my shoulders

pigeons

all

in a flash

under one

tree

                    turning
and the light's the farthest point
of the road

why see you
other than
perfect woman
moving gently
along stream
thru wood

newest rage
click-clack
      cicada

flying against a window
falling three stories
a bird
former life
a man
sensible
foolish
no less

a whole garden of angels
each leaning upon each
light flowering heavenward
tho each flower heaven
animals under flame
key releasing ground
fire air earth water
outside the walls

leaving the airport
taking the bus
riding past cemetery
thru shopping district
the city truer
              dustier
the guest gone

shucking our bathing suits

the little window
above the sink
blinding

you pass a
couchant black cat
to the left
of a stoop

you say
no reason
to give it
a second
thought

then
late night
disaster

Golden maiden in a brazen tower
Behold Jupiter his golden shower

after supper in Chinatown
we walked home along the Bowery
our attention
quickened by a crash
somebody put a rock
or something or other
thru a shop window
then ran up the stairs
of the hotel
a few doors down

climbing the subway steps
hearing a bird in the tree
behind the shoeshine stand
the rush hour crowd
equally awakening

isolation

grass
along
a river
in shadow

feeling space as something solid
estranging the body from its object
the soul seeing thru
remaining ingathered
biding its time

ghostly
petals
whirling
about

offsetting
shaded
walk

haunt
even
waking
dream

when I got off the bus there she was
I hadn't seen her for almost 3 wks
we walked up a ways to the cottage

moonlight in the room
our bodies exhausted from loving
we lay talking
sleep surprising

a couple on a bench
their kids over
by the sand pile
even tho rain
any minute

listening to the world outside

the soul in the body doing the same thing

therefore a room still somewhat outside

```
curving the road
                overlooking
a lake

other cars
         alongside
contributing

to
  the
symmetry
```

longing for purity
finding onself
instead
a wanderer
amidst
      at the edge of
green

curving the road
             overlooking
a lake

other cars
          alongside
contributing

to
  the
symmetry

longing for purity
finding onself
instead
a wanderer
amidst
      at the edge of
green

a few feet from the water
by a path
a bench

the house behind the grove
half way up the hill
linking highway to cove

separating husband and wife
the sea makes pillars of both
their gaze oned by vertex

whether hill
or plain
skyline
seemingly
sea

evening light the whole length of trees
the rest of the forest
                    impenetrably
                                dark

in a clearing
in a wood
at twilight
a family

walking about
gathering
strange enough
driftwood

imagine a cliff
with a lighthouse
a ways back
and a storm
rumling
        and
                crackling
at its very
          crest

counterbalanced
by the shade
half light
half dark
        a lilac sprig
        in the vase
        on the window sill

lie up on a slope
untrapped by metaphor

a turn around the city
but if the streets
show degeneration
then no cruise
can alter that fact
despite the guide
speaking directly
to the out-of-towners
and the foreigners

the tree in the line of our vision
in light
        tho every other tree
of the park
        dark

Then the dwelling of the angel in the soul
or rather the odor
sign
of the dwelling
continuing
habituating the man
to the daily
drawing out radiance
preparing
rendering
transparent
the surroundings
the universe
the aureole
receiving
truest
ray

each facet light accordingly
the souls responding
orienting
becoming
together
perfect
gem

body in grass
elliptically formed
in turn inscribed
in square
in flame
flower
center
sustained
by
four
angels

Disigilla

from the distance of a return home
an evocation of a walk thru the city
the flow of people characteristic
the pilgrim secure upon the waters

climbing stairs
dread accruing
the sense
····unceasing mentation
the oddity
····speech

leaning against a tree
the left foot by a path
the incline abrupt
a marsh from thereon
                        out

water lilies
            and the reflection
bridge
bride
bridegroom

the more
distant
the wood
the river
the valley
the more
encompassing
the bird
spiraling

not a projection
but an apparition
a body
standing amidst

a crowded train
the counterpart
sitting by the doors
head bowed
eyes closed

stepping out from under willow
river close by

        ascending order

        wooded hillside
        ocean
        setting sun

archway hung with roses
garden
    here
        cut hedges
    there
        tombstone
light
    and
        haze
clinging
      even
          to
blades
    of
        grass

the windows no different from night
even so   books disarrayed on a chest of draws
          quasi end table
          and a lamp
                  lowly lit

a refrain

my love in a blue dress
passes a white bench
and the lilac bush
              behind it

proving ground

they came to the eastside
making their mark

scattering afterwards
buying farms or cottages

while one or two others maybe
unknown to each other
continue to roam city

finding out a generation later
old news
a newspaper partly in slush

at the foot
of a block
of turn-of-the-century
tenements

a great bridge
leading up
or falling off
to nowhere

lying on a stone
the palm of a hand
a tree
      specifically branches in snow
                                        by them
the lovers in dream ogle the corner
across the street and to the left
of the clock tower

standing in grove
no frame of reference
space rather
        or
                effluvium

love	knowledge	divided
mysticism	science	divided
union	identity	divided
glorified body	spiritual man	undivided

the day drab
meeting the buildings
all the way

tempted to buy
a bunch of roses
from a vender
at a popular
intersection

proper perspective
the sidereal
the intangible

total effect

gray sky

two streaks of light

five buildings

the bare branches
of the trees
of one
of the bounding lines
of the square

if a man wakes sprightly
the body
not necessarily
diaphanous

if heavily
possibly
earth
by degrees

glorifying

the heart skips a beat
when the sun withdraws

something like a fall

an elevator from the 15th
to the 1st
without a stop

observe the body
              for signs
                            of spiritualization

                            if translucent
                            then icebergs
                            float outward
                            dissolving at horizon

the eye goes toward the ceiling
especially the corners

nothing

leaving the apartment
same sound
in the hallway
                the fluttering   the corners

duality is rhythm   the essence of duality is rhythm

the essence or nature of rhythm is duality
positive and negative poles alternating indefinitely
the inner structure indefinite total combination

Afterword

Those who have found Frank Samperi's work tend to remember what brought them to it: a chance citing on a bookshelf, a friend, a fortuitous accident. The memory of what engendered the encounter with Samperi's poetry is indelible because this poetry is itself indelible. It haunts; Samperi's poetry, though it sometimes includes what may seem to be mundane detail, is not for the casual reader. It is made of (and demands) attention that turns toward transformation, and on, toward the transcendent.

One of the powers that Samperi's poetry exerts over the reader is its deep humanity. One sees him loving his wife and his children, grimly absorbing the urban scape, suffering with despair and isolation. Just as vividly, the poet rejoices at the renewals of the natural world and partakes of wonder. That Samperi so acutely feels and sometimes anguishes over the limitations of self and circumstance makes the fortitude of his faith only more telling. I am reminded of Simone Weil's thinking about affliction and its redemptive power:

> It is only necessary to know that love is a direction and not a state of the soul. If one is unaware of this, one falls into despair at the first onslaught of affliction.
>
> He whose soul remains ever turned toward God though the nail pierces it finds himself nailed to the very center of the universe. It is the true center; it is not in the middle; it is beyond space and time; it is God. In a dimension that does not belong to space, that is not time, that is indeed quite a different dimension, this nail has pierced cleanly through all creation, through the thickness of the screen separating the soul from God.[1]

What occurs at this site, Weil observes, is "the intersection of creation and its Creator." Attuned in this way to an ultimate "intersection," Samperi is enabled to witness to the quietest, seemingly most inconsequential moments as evidence of a larger grace unfolding. "Come here," he gestures, "by this window—

---

1. Simon Weil, *Waiting for God* (New York: G. P. Putnam and Sons, 1951), pp. 135–36.

look, / Up there, the sun has become inconstant." That is, the divine registers even in the "drift" (a recurring work in the Samperi lexicon) of human perception. Some pages later, Samperi, who is fascinated by light—as illumination of the mind, as a measure of movement and time, as divine presence—writes, "It is better, I mean, to be here, / Where the mind can act / And make light where there is none."

The intersection, thus, between creation and Creator, looks teleologically toward the sufficiency and surfeit of the divine. And so Frank Samperi, too, looks insistently, orienting himself anew in poem after poem, to a direction and not a state of the soul, that anticipates and passionately desires union with divine totality:

> but when the writing has reached
> its final word
> the word reduces itself
> to closed word
> the closed word raised to another height
> only if another extension is seen
> which extension in turn
> imparts
> to everything that went before
> the vision

The definitive vision, as conveyed in this body of work, is both true and elusive. Samperi chafes against "the Material Ideal," the realm of worldly acclaim and its illusory rewards. The speaker of these poems is sometimes deeply lonely, misunderstood, exhausted by the demands of work and his Work. "My revolt," he states emphatically, "is not to give in / to any desire / that ultimately leads / to a justification." Desire and its vision must suffice. Though the nail of human experience pierces him, he turns again and yet again toward God. In the inconstancy of the light toward which he turns (or better, perhaps, the fallibility of human apprehension of such light), he slowly transforms himself into a conduit for the vision:

> the window
> looks
> and sees

This process entails taking the greatest risks. The transparency of the window may disclose a view that no other viewer could share. Samperi negotiates this gap by bringing his human attention to bear in precise, original, and sometimes even whimsical ways. Among my favorites, this slightly wry, but still affirmative piece stands out:

> Taking
> the train
> back to Brooklyn—
>
> thinking
> always day
> posits
> your intent
>
> in the
> renewing
> as in
> the old—
>
> my loneliness
> greets
> a friendly
> world
>
> even
> the painted
> sign
> on a factory
>
> wall:
> House
> of the
> Dairymaid.

The playfulness of "House / of the / Dairymaid" lingers, but at the same time acquires a kind of iconographic holiness that transmutes loneliness by way of the hospitality offered by a friendly world. Subway and factory become a means by which the poet deliberately orients himself within a holy vision, "your intent / / in the / renewing."

Flannery O'Connor who was, like Samperi, a consciously Catholic writer, wrote that when writing is written "according to its nature, it should reinforce our sense of the supernatural by grounding it in concrete, observable reality. If the writer uses his eyes in the real security of this Faith, he will be obliged to use them honestly, and his sense of mystery, and acceptance of it, will be increased."[2] I can think of no poet who manages this crossroads more subtly and adeptly than Samperi. His very modesty is the sign of his deep concentration on the given, material world as it is charged with divine overflow. I read his poems repeatedly yet am each time caught in the suspension that he creates, the difficult recognition of mortal fragmentation as it reaches toward fulfillment. This is the precariousness that faith necessitates. O'Connor asserts that the writer presents a mystery, "grace through nature, but when he finishes there always has to be left over that sense of Mystery which cannot be accounted for by any human formula" (153). In his introduction to this publication, Peter O'Leary writes aptly that Samperi's poetry is "laden with divine messages and abiding in a realm that intermediates the worldly and the heavenly." Those of us who come to value and study Frank Samperi's poetry do so because we take part in the recognition that is a primary element of spirituality. We do not own or control meaning, but we orient ourselves to its mystery. Samperi's poetry intermediates the gap between the known and the unknowable, the grief of mortality and the desire that unifies belief with what transcends it:

love	knowledge	divided
mysticism	science	divided
union	identity	divided
glorified body	spiritual man	undivided

—Elizabeth Robinson, August 2012

---

2. Flannery O'Connor, *Mystery and Manners* (New York: Farrar, Strauss and Giroux, 1961), p. 150.

Appendix

Jacket note to *Quadrifarim*:

The poet writes of the first two volumes:

> The relationship bears a single experience, *One of the Intelligences*, that is, at one end implied (*The Prefiguration*), at the other established (*Quadrifariam*), therefore, the emotion *companionship*: however, *Quadrifariam* carries with it the descent, *book, canzone, song*, that is, *Eternity, Image, Gift*, which is to say that the *collapse* gets defined in a more detailed manner ...
>
> "The Triune" (first book of the present volume [i.e., *Quadrifariam*] seeks to fulfill Aquinas' sense of St. Hilary's "Eternity is the Father, the species is in the Image, and use is in the Gift," and more specifically to resolve epical desire, that is, delineate book, canzone, song, only in the end to let go, release boundary. Of course, all this bears upon the deeper generalization: "Quadrifariam" means fourfold, but this meaning carries with it Aquinas' sense of Augustine's, both bearing upon Dante's—the spiritual refrain of the work. In other words, "The Triune" is the theme throughout, the title presenting the paradox: foundation yet boundaries released ... The titles (of the books of the volumes) are not without meaning—one could comparee them to *steps*, the more inclusive title reorienting them, the more inclusive in turn looking toward the other inclusive, the third and final volume, *the crown*, the state, union identity at rest, part and parcel of all three, the unitive title foregone, spiritual man state before the Mystery.
>
> ... hard to get at a gist of what I think is a gist: one sings in order to get away from explanation.

A Note on the Text

The three books collected in this volume were originally published in the early 1970s by Mushinsha/Grossman and were, in many cases, gatherings of earlier small press work by the author.

The present collection retains, as far as possible, the large format of the Mushinsha/Grossman books, as well as the many blank pages which pepper the text. Page numbers—missing from the originals and from other works published during the author's lifetime—have been added sparingly to aid readers and to encourage the exegesis Frank Samperi's poetry so richly deserves.

www.ingramcontent.com/pod-product-compliance
Lightning Source LLC
Chambersburg PA
CBHW080537230426
43663CB00015B/2619